*FM 55-1

Field Manual
No. 55-1

Headquarters
Department of the Army
Washington, DC, 3 October 1995

TRANSPORTATION OPERATIONS

Contents

Distribution Restriction: Approved for public release; distribution is unlimited.

*This publication supersedes FM 55-1, 30 November 1984.

Preface

This manual provides standards for the execution of Army transportation functions in support of military operations. It reflects the shift to joint operations, prompted by the 1986 Goldwater-Nichols Act. It presents the transportation doctrine commanders require to integrate the Army's transportation capability with the capabilities of other Services and the DTS. This doctrine applies when executing missions throughout the full range of military operations, including OOTW. It is also applicable regardless of the size of the Army force involved in an operation.

The manual portrays the Army transportation system as a basic element of warfighting. It uses the strategic, operational, and tactical levels of war to frame the system. Because the system is controlled by different commands throughout the levels, this manual describes procedures commanders should follow to establish a seamless total distribution system. The system links all Army installations, to include forts, camps, mobilization stations, and depots to fighting positions. This manual uses the functions of a transportation system to present the Army transportation capabilities. These elements are movements control, terminal operations, and mode operations.

The primary users of this manual are ASCC and their staffs. The manual is also useful to senior Army, joint service and allied officers serving as joint/combined force commanders or staff officers, and noncommissioned officers. It also contains guidance to handle the requirements generated by other governmental and non-governmental agencies, as well as HN elements, involved in the operation. Moreover, the manual is designed to assist other Service component commanders in their understanding of the Army's transportation capability. Finally, all military leaders will find this manual useful in their general professional education.

This manual implements pertinent doctrine from joint publications. These publications include Joint Pub 4.0, Joint Pub 4.01.1, Joint Pub 4.01.2, Joint Pub 4.01.3, and Joint Pub 4.01.5. It is fully compatible with the Army doctrine contained in FM 100-5 and supports the contents of FM 100-7, FM 100-8, FM 100-10, and FM 100-16. This manual also recognizes the doctrine contained in FM 100-17 and FM 100-19.

The proponent of this publication is HQ TRADOC. Submit changes for improving this publication on DA Form 2028 (Recommended Changes to Publications and Blank Forms) and forward it to Commandant, US Army Transportation School, ATTN: ATSP-TDX, Fort Eustis, VA 23604-5389.

Unless this publication states otherwise, masculine nouns and pronouns do not refer exclusively to men.

Chapter 1

Fundamentals of Transportation Operations

Need lead in when this FM is updated.

TRANSPORTATION AND THE NATIONAL MILITARY STRATEGY

1-1. The foundations of the national military strategy derive from the national security strategy. This strategy places four fundamental demands on the US military. These demands are:

- Ensuring strategic deterrence and defense.
- Exercising forward presence in vital areas.
- Responding effectively to crisis.
- Retaining the national capacity to reconstitute forces.

1-2. As the principal land warfare component of the Armed Forces of the US, the Army plays a vital role in fulfilling these demands. In turn, an expansible and adaptable transportation system (see Figure 1-1, page 1-2) plays a key role in the Army's capabilities to fulfill each demand. A responsive and capable transportation system adds credibility to the US strategic deterrence capability and sustains the forward presence forces. The transportation system also plays a key role in projecting and supporting the reconstitution of the force.

1-3. The synchronized execution of the transportation functions reinforce the capability to conduct military operations. These functions are movement control (sometimes called traffic management), terminal operations, and mode operations. These functions are defined below.

MOVEMENT CONTROL

1-4. Movement control is the planning, routing, scheduling, controlling, coordinating, and ITV of personnel, units, equipment, and supplies moving over LOC. It involves the commitment of allocated transportation assets and the acquisition of HN transportation services to support military operations. Its goal is to optimize common-user transportation modes and terminals. This effort links common-user assets with the organic transportation capabilities of the supported units. Common-user transportation assets support the whole force. Movement control is the linchpin of a transportation system.

TERMINAL OPERATIONS

1-5. Terminal operations is the staging, loading, discharge, transfer handling, and documentation of cargo or personnel between various transport modes. The two major groups that exist are water terminal and inland terminal operations.

1-6. Water terminals consist of fixed ports, unimproved ports, or bare beaches. Inland terminals consist of air, inland water, rail, highway, or petroleum terminals. Logistic planners at all levels must provide for the adequate manning of terminals. They must also provide for suitable facilities to ease the handling of the scheduled mode(s) and types of cargo and personnel.

MODE OPERATIONS

1-7. Mode operations use transportation assets to link terminals into a continuous movements chain. The two major modes are surface and air. The surface mode is further subdivided into sea, inland waterway, highway, rail, and pipeline modes. The air mode is subdivided into fixed-wing and rotary-wing modes.

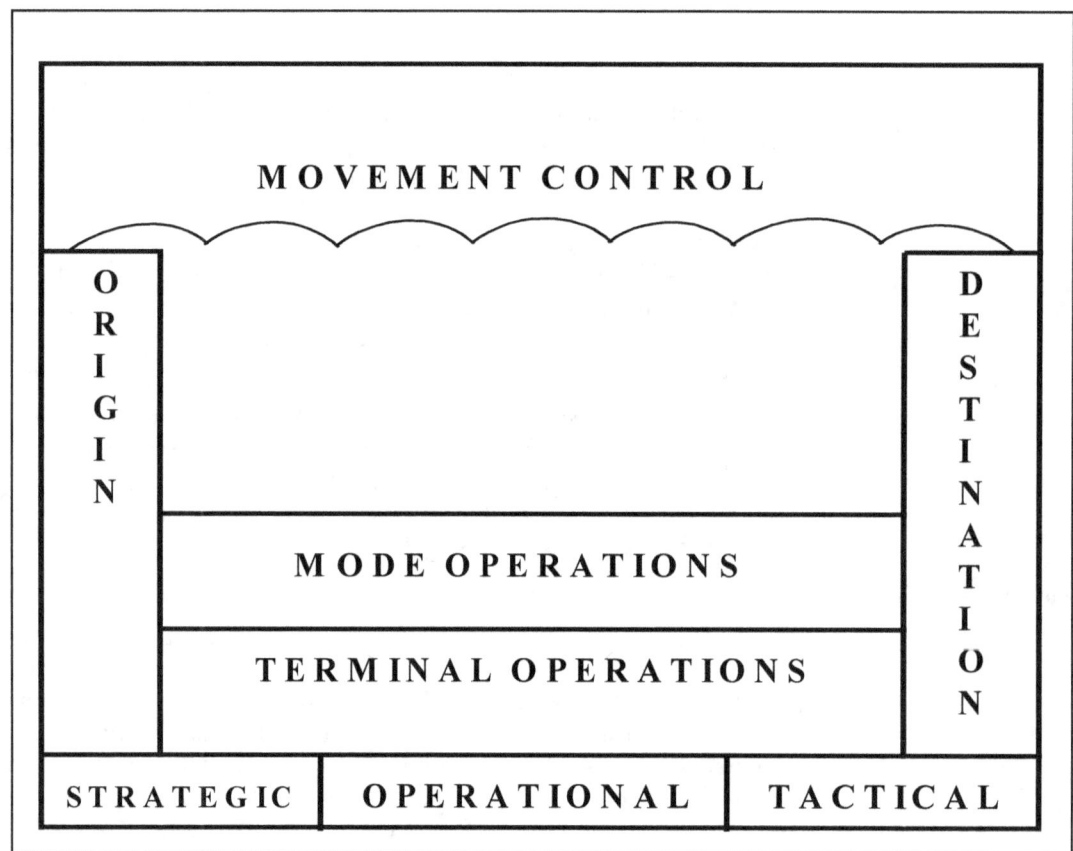

Figure 1-1. The Transportation System

MAJOR INFLUENCES ON MILITARY OPERATIONS

1-8. Three major factors influence how military planners structure a transportation system to support a military operation. These factors are the levels of war, the range of military operations, and the political nature of the US involvement. Army planners, working in a joint environment or in an Army component command, must understand the relationships between these factors. The planners must identify the transportation function and determine at which level of war to place the function. The planners must also identify the type of military operation and the nature of the US involvement. Considering these factors and their relationships will clarify requirements and help establish the transportation system needed to support the operation.

THE LEVELS OF WAR

1-9. FM 100-5 defines the three levels of war as strategic, operational, and tactical. These levels exist in every military operation regardless of the size of the committed force. Commanders at each of the levels can also be readily identified for each operation. FM 100-5 also defines the levels of war more by the consequences of their outcome than by the echelon of involvement. This means, it is not always easy to distinguish between a strategic, operational, or tactical action. At times, strategic organizations conduct activities within the operational commander's AOR. The opposite can also occur. Often defining the type of military action properly will be more helpful in determining where to conduct the activity within the AO. However, as a general rule, the higher the echelon of command, the higher the level of war. The levels of war influence how the military approaches the range of military operations and the links to establish between tactical actions and strategic objectives.

THE RANGE OF MILITARY OPERATIONS

1-10. The Army is required to function through a range of military operations. The range spans three states (from peacetime, through conflict, to war). The Army calls its activities during peacetime and conflict OOTW. Like the levels of war, the dividing lines between the components of the range of military operations are not discrete and are difficult to define. For example, the Army may find itself operating in all three states at the same time and in one or more regions of the world. Also, during the conduct of a military operation, changes between the states may occur. The range of military operations requires a well planned and organized robust transportation force structure.

1-11. Military planners must identify and tailor transportation organizations to fit the type of military operation. It is also important for military planners to integrate and coordinate all plans so they mutually support strategic objectives. This is not an easy undertaking. Often the US involvement requires the military to work with forces and private organizations from other nations, adding complexity to the tasks. Figure 1-2, page 1-4, portrays the range of military operations in a theater strategic environment.

STATES OF THE ENVIRONMENTS	GOAL	MILITARY OPERATIONS			EXAMPLES
WAR	Fight and Win	War			Large-scale combat operations
			C	N	Attack
			O	O	Defend
CONFLICT	Deter War and Resolve Conflict	Other Than War	M	N	Strikes and raids
			B	C	Peace enforcement
			A	O	Support to insurgency
			T	M	Antiterrorism
				B	Peacekeeping
					NEO
PEACETIME	Promote Peace	Other Than War		A	Counterdrug
				T	Disaster relief
					Civil support
					Peace building
					Nation assistance

The states of peacetime, conflict, and war could all exist at once in the theater commander's strategic environment. He can respond to requirements with a wide range of military operations. Noncombat operations might occur during war, just as some OOTW might require combat.

Figure 1-2. Range of Military Operations in the Theater Strategic Environment

THE POLITICAL NATURE OF THE US INVOLVEMENT

1-12. Political conditions will influence the nature of any US involvement. The three possible conditions consist of the following:

- The US acting alone.

- The US acting with one or more allies.

- The US acting as a part of an international organization, such as the UN and NATO.

Each of the political conditions has implications for the transportation system. Each operation will require the tailoring of transportation forces and, if required, the melding of support received from other nations and organizations. Knowledge of the system and force structure tailoring will provide the capability to meet the US commitment.

THE DEFENSE TRANSPORTATION SYSTEM

1-13. The DTS supports all military operations. It is that portion of the nation's transportation infrastructure which supports DOD transportation needs through the range of military operations. The DTS, in turn, operates as an integral part of the national transportation system.

1-14. The DTS consists of military and commercial assets, services, and systems that are organic, contracted, or controlled by DOD. Operating the DTS involves the management of a complex number of interrelationships within the DOD and among diverse federal and commercial activities. All military transportation activities, regardless of the function they execute, must follow the programs and policies of the DTS.

1-15. When planning support for military operations, military transportation planners and operators at the joint and Service level must consider the diversity of the DTS and its accompanying coordinating challenges. Planners must also understand that DOD policy allows government intervention into the private sector only to the degree necessary to ensure the civil transportation system is responsive to military needs. This means DOD activates private sector assets to augment DTS capabilities only to meet the shortfalls of the defense transportation capacity. Figure 1-3, page 1-6, shows the organizations that form the DTS. Chapter 2 contains the roles and responsibilities of the agencies that make up the DTS. Joint Publication 4-01 contains a thorough discussion of the DTS.

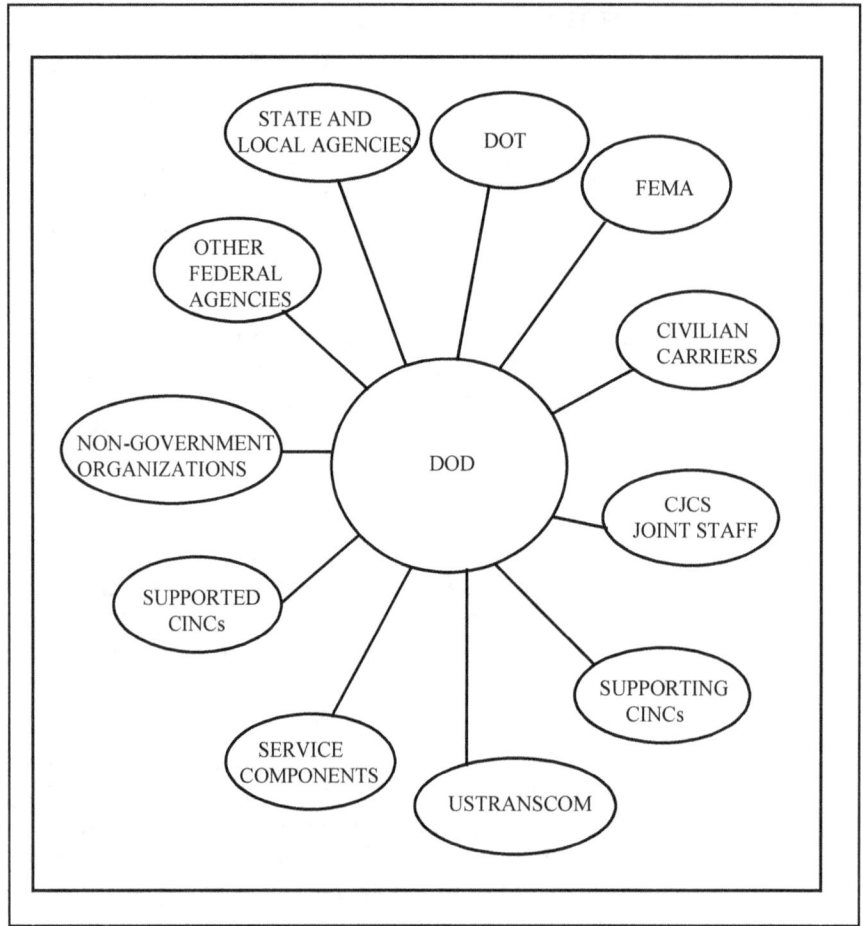

Figure 1-3. Defense Transportation System Supporting Organizations

THE ARMY TRANSPORTATION SYSTEM

1-16. To comply with its Title 10 US Code responsibilities, the Army organizes, trains, and equips organizations to execute the Army transportation mission. These organizations consist of military units that provide movement control and operate terminals and modes. The Army designs, trains, and equips its transportation organizations to fit into the levels of war, range of military operations, and the political nature of US involvement. These organizations form a transportation system that spans the levels of war and operates on a daily peacetime basis. The system is designed to integrate its activities with the larger DTS. It is also expandable and tailorable to meet the increased surge requirements of a contingency. It relies on active duty and RC units and may use multinational, HN, or contract support.

ARMY TRANSPORTATION AT THE STRATEGIC LEVEL OF WAR

1-17. Because of the nature of the strategic level of war, a joint environment dominates the execution of the transportation functions. At this level, DOD provides the programs and policies the USTRANSCOM executes. USTRANSCOM provides strategic movement control and operates strategic airlift and sealift. USTRANSCOM also operates terminals designated as POE when the deployment or sustainment starts in CONUS. USTRANSCOM may also operate terminals within the AO of combatant commands through negotiated agreements. Combatant commands and USTRANSCOM manage the strategic deployment of forward deployed units. In executing the functions of the transportation system at the strategic level, USTRANSCOM works with the Joint Staff, the Service departments, and the combatant commands and their Service components.

1-18. At the strategic level, Army transportation personnel man movement control staff positions in joint and Service component HQ. Army transportation organizations also operate or help operate terminals designated as POEs, and operate or administer contracted or HN acquired assets. The main Army organizations responsible for these functions within CONUS are the MTMC and the FORSCOM. MTMC is the Army component of USTRANSCOM. FORSCOM is the Army component for the USACOM. For forward deployed forces, the main Army organization responsible for transportation functions is the ASCC. The focus of Army transportation personnel and organizations at the strategic level is to assist the Army in meeting the joint force requirements in the following areas:

- Mobilization.
- Requirements Determination.
- Acquisition.
- Stockpiling.
- Army Reserve Stocks.
- Deployment/Redeployment.
- Reconstitution.
- Demobilization.
- Doctrine and Force Design and Development.

ARMY TRANSPORTATION AT THE OPERATIONAL LEVEL OF WAR

1-19. At the operational level of war, transportation functions remain joint; but to a lesser degree than at the strategic level. The execution of operational level transportation functions is the responsibility of operational level commanders, who are usually JFCs. The JFC normally retains overall movement control responsibilities through the creation of a JTB, a JMC, or both. However, the JFC usually delegates the operation of terminals and modes to the Service components, while retaining authority to establish priorities and ensuring unity of effort among the Service components. JFCs also perform duties at the strategic level of war when they are tasked to deploy forces outside their AOR.

1-20. At the operational level of war, the ASCC assumes responsibility for transportation and establishes an operational level of war transportation system. The system includes staff personnel, movement control organizations, and a capability to operate Army terminals and modes. It also acquires and oversees the operation of HN or contracted assets, as required. It also supports other Services or allies, as necessary, or as directed by the JFC. Army transportation personnel at this level direct their focus to assist the ASCC in meeting responsibilities in the following areas:

- Deployment/Repositioning of Forces.
- Reception and Onward Movement of the Force.
- Positioning of Facilities.
- Movements Control.
- Distribution.
- Reconstitution.
- Redeployment.

ARMY TRANSPORTATION AT THE TACTICAL LEVEL OF WAR

1-21. At the tactical level of war, the responsibility for transportation operations belongs to the tactical commander. At this level, Army transportation support normally directs its efforts to the committed Army forces. However, as directed by the tactical commander, the system may provide support to other Services and allies.

1-22. At the tactical level of war the Army may field a corps, a division, or a brigade. Each of these organizations has organic elements that provide for staff transportation support, movement control operations, and terminal and mode operations. The Army Corps, Division, and the Brigade commanders, using assigned resources, establish the tactical level Army transportation system. At this level, the Army may also field a task force tailored to meet the specific requirements of the operation. An example is a task force made up of logistic units designed to provide humanitarian assistance. Movements control, terminal operations, and mode operations organizations would be assigned to the task force to meet the specific requirements. Regardless of its organization, the Army tactical transportation system provides final distribution of personnel and materiel. The focus of this support is in the following areas:

- Arming.
- Fueling.
- Fixing.
- Moving.
- Manning.
- Sustaining the Soldier.

Chapter 2

Roles and Responsibilities

Need lead in when this FM is updated.

INTRODUCTION

2-1. This chapter identifies the roles and responsibilities for the execution of transportation functions within DOD. The US military executes these functions under the umbrella of the DTS. This chapter also contains a discussion of non-DOD organizations that support the DTS when required.

2-2. To add to the DOD organic capability, many organizations provide transportation support to the Armed Forces of the US. These organizations include federal, state, and local agencies; the private sector within the US under contract agreements; foreign governments under HNS arrangements; and contracted foreign private industry.

DEPARTMENT OF DEFENSE

2-3. At the apex of the DTS is DOD. DOD includes the Office of the Secretary of Defense, the Joint Chiefs of Staff, the Joint Staff, Defense agencies, DOD field activities, military departments and military services within those departments, combatant commands, and other organizations and activities that may be established or designated by law, the President, or the Secretary of Defense. The combatant commands have regional or functional responsibilities. Figure 2-1, page 2-1, shows the combatant command organization. USACOM, in addition to its regional responsibilities, is responsible for joint training, readiness of CONUS based forces for deployment, and force packaging in support of other regional combatant commanders. USTRANSCOM has the functional, global responsibility for transportation.

2-4. Within DOD, the SECDEF is responsible for planning and executing transportation operations. This responsibility includes operating the DTS. The Deputy Undersecretary of Defense (Logistics) executes transportation operations for the SECDEF. The Undersecretary accomplishes this responsibility by publishing DOD directives, memorandums, instructions, and regulations, and by sponsoring the development of multiservice transportation regulations. AR 55-355/NAVSUPINST 4600.70/AFR 75-2/MCO P460.14B/DLAR 4500.3, a multiservice regulation, provides procedures that govern DTS actions. Joint Pub 4-01 covers the interface requirements between the Services and the DTS.

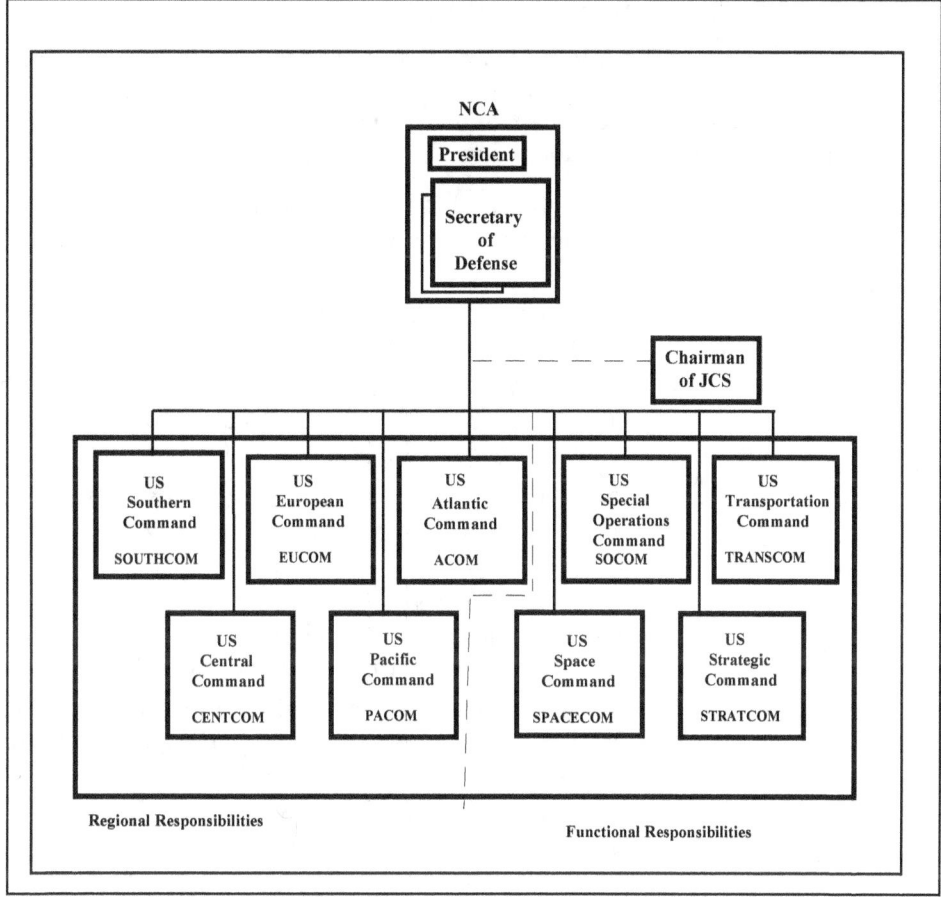

Figure 2-1. Combatant Command Organization

THE JOINT CHIEFS OF STAFF

2-5. The JCS consists of the Chairman, the Vice Chairman, the Chief of Staff of the Army, the Chief of Naval Operations, the Chief of Staff of the Air Force, and the Commandant of the Marine Corps. The President and the SECDEF make up the NCA.

2-6. The Goldwater-Nichols DOD Reorganization Act of 1986 reinforced the operational chain of command. The command line runs from the President to the SECDEF to the combatant commanders. It also established the CJCS as the principal military advisor to the NCA and NSC. All communications between the NCA and the combatant CINCs pass through the CJCS unless otherwise directed by the NCA. However, all JCS members are individually, by law, military advisors, and may respond to a request or voluntarily submit advice or opinions to the President, SECDEF, or the NSC. The advice or opinions made by the CJCS or individual members of the JCS may include transportation matters.

THE CHAIRMAN OF THE JOINT CHIEFS OF STAFF

2-7. The CJCS transportation role is primarily strategic in nature. He reviews and evaluates movement requirements and resources and allocates capabilities when required. The CJCS responsibilities includes the following:

- Managing JOPES, which includes establishing procedures for the submission of movement requirements by DOD user components to USTRANSCOM.

- Establishing procedures for USTRANSCOM to evaluate requirements and movement capabilities.

- Assuring procedures are established in coordination with the proper Assistant Secretary of Defense and the Secretaries of the military departments.

- Prescribing a movement priority system that will ensure responsiveness to meet the requirements of the using forces.

- Monitoring the capabilities of USTRANSCOM common-user transportation resources to provide airlift, sealift, CONUS land transportation, and common-user ocean terminal service based upon the requirements of DOD components.

- Assigning movement priorities to support requirements of DOD user components based upon capabilities reported by USTRANSCOM.

- Apportioning and/or allocating strategic lift assets.

THE JOINT STAFF

2-8. The Joint Staff supports the CJCS. Its directorates coordinate specific functional areas, including transportation. The main staff element involved in coordinating transportation matters is the J4. This staff office has the primary responsibility for strategic transportation and for the operation of the JTB.

JOINT TRANSPORTATION BOARD

2-9. The JTB acts for the CJCS by directing or recommending courses of action concerning priorities and allocations for the use of airlift, sealift, and surface transportation capability. The JTB watches the balance between DOD transportation requirements and capabilities through close liaison with the combatant command CINCs. The USCINCTRANS monitors strategic transportation requirements and capabilities for the JTB. The USCINCTRANS also provides transportation based on the movement requirements established by the CJCS, the Chiefs of the Services, and the CINCs. The USCINCTRANS refers problems in the balance between transportation requirements and capabilities to the JTB for resolution. A recommendation usually goes with the referral of the problem.

2-10. The Joint Staff Vice Director for Logistics chairs the JTB. Voting members of the JTB are general/flag rank officers from the Operations, Plans and Policy, and Plans and Interoperability Directorates of the Joint Staff and the Service logistics/transportation staffs. USTRANSCOM provides permanent nonvoting representatives to inform and advise the JTB.

THE COMBATANT COMMAND STRUCTURE

GUIDE TO TERMINOLOGY

The terms "unified command," "specified command," and "combatant command" refer to commands established by the President as combatant commands under Title 10, United States Code, section 161. The acronym "CINC," which means commander in chief, refers to the commander of a combatant command.

Addition of the word "geographic" to a CINC or commander describes a combatant commander of a unified command that includes a general geographic area of responsibility. Similarly, adding the word "functional" to CINC or commander, describes a combatant commander of a unified command with functional responsibilities.

The term "joint force commander" is used in a generic sense to refer to the commander of a combatant command, subordinate unified command, or a joint task force.

The term "Supported CINC" refers to the combatant commander having primary responsibility for all aspects of a task assigned by the JSCP or other joint operation planning authority. The "Supporting CINC," on the the other hand, provides augmentation forces or other support to a designated supported commander or commanders.

2-11. The combatant commands are the unified and specified commands established by the President, through the Secretary of Defense with the advice and assistance of the Chairman, Joint Chiefs of Staff. A unified command is a command with a broad continuing mission under a single commander and is composed of significant assigned components of two or more Services. A specified command is a command that has a broad continuing mission and is composed of forces from but one Service. (There are no specified commands at this time.)

2-12. Combatant commanders exercise COCOM (command authority) over assigned forces and are directly responsible to the NCA for the performance of assigned missions and the preparedness of their commands. COCOM is vested only in the commanders of combatant commands and cannot be delegated or transferred. It is the authority of a combatant commander to perform those functions of command involving organizing and employing commands and forces, assigning tasks, designating objectives, and giving authoritative direction over all aspects of military operations, joint training, and logistics necessary to accomplish the missions assigned to the command.

2-13. In the area of logistics, combatant commanders may exercise directive authority. The exercise of directive authority for logistics includes the authority to issue directives to subordinate commanders necessary to ensure the following: effective execution of approved operation plans, effectiveness and economy of operation, and prevention or elimination of unnecessary duplication of facilities and overlapping of functions among the Service component commands.

2-14. Under crisis action, wartime conditions or where critical situations make diversion of the normal logistic process necessary, the logistic and administrative authority of combatant commanders enable them to use all facilities and supplies of all forces assigned to their commands as necessary for the accomplishment of their missions.

2-15. Commanders of unified commands may establish subordinate unified commands when so authorized by the Secretary of Defense through the Chairman of the Joint Chiefs of Staff. Combatant commanders may also establish joint task forces to execute specific missions.

SUPPORTED COMBATANT COMMANDER

2-16. The NCA allocates forces to supported CINCs to meet assigned missions. These forces include transportation organizations. During peacetime operations, CINCs follow the procedures contained in Joint Pub 4-01 and AR 55-355/NAVSUPINST 4600.70/AFR 75-2/MCO P460.14B/DLAR 4500.3 to use DTS assets. When the CINC executes a force projection or reinforcement mission, he has the following transportation responsibilities:

- Exercising combatant command authority over assigned forces.

- Exercising directive authority over logistics to maintain effectiveness and economy of operations and to prevent duplication of resources.

- Coordinating with USTRANSCOM and supporting CINCs in executing the TPFDL and assuring the availability of transportation resources to support the deployment of the force.

- Establishing a transportation system to support the forward presence or deployed force within the AO.

- Establishing priorities to move deploying units and their sustainment.

- Validating strategic movements.

- Using JOPES to manage the development of plans, to include the deployment of the force.

- Establishing a JTB or JMC, to act as the CINC's executive agent for transportation.

- Ensuring that the departure and arrival of transportation organizations are sequenced to provide support to units that have yet to deploy and sustainment to those already forward.

- Providing adequate and assured communications to movement control organizations.

SUPPORTING CINCS OTHER THAN USCINCTRANS

2-17. Supporting CINCs provide the support and resources required by the JSCP, approved war plans, and NCA direction. This support may be in the form of provision of forces and materiel, much in the same way that the EUCOM supported CENTCOM during Operation Desert Shield/Desert Storm. Agreements between CINCs may also influence the support. Examples are: CAAs, CMAAs, and MOUs. In the area of transportation, supporting CINCs have the following responsibilities:

- Exercising combatant command over assigned forces.

- Coordinating with the supported CINC and USTRANSCOM to assure the command provides support based on the priorities of the supported CINC.

- Using JOPES to manage the development of plans to include the deployment of the force in coordination with the supported CINC.

- Establishing or expanding the existing transportation system within his AOR.

- Establishing or expanding movement control operations to manage the execution of supporting transportation tasks.

- Operating the modes and the terminals used as POE by the deploying organizations, when the force is forward deployed.

UNITED STATES TRANSPORTATION COMMAND

2-18. USTRANSCOM, as the DOD single manager for transportation and a supporting combatant command, provides air, land, and sea transportation to meet national security objectives through the range of military operations. USTRANSCOM orchestrates all transportation aspects of planning and execution with the Joint Staff and the appropriate combatant and Service commands. USTRANSCOM has the following responsibilities:

- Exercising combatant command authority over the TCCs. The TCCs are AMC, MTMC, and MSC.
- Coordinating global air, land, and sea transportation planning in support of CINCs, through JOPES. These responsibilities include:
  - During deliberate planning, providing CINCs with the coordinated transportation expertise required to complete capabilities-based operations plans. USTRANSCOM continues to provide assistance in periodic plan maintenance efforts.
  - During CAP, providing deployment estimates and total lift asset availability to the NCA and supported CINCs. Supported CINCs use this data to develop courses of action and optimal flow of forces.
  - During deployment execution, acts like a JMC for the Joint Staff and the NCA.

Air Mobility Command

2-19. AMC is a major command of the US Air Force. It provides common-user airlift transportation services to deploy, employ, and sustain US forces on a global basis. AMC is also responsible for strategic medical evacuation and manages the CRAF when DOD activates these assets. It also manages civilian chartered flights, when they support a military operation. Joint Pub 4-01.1 contains more information on the operations of AMC.

Military Sealift Command

2-20. MSC is a major command of the US Navy. It provides common-user sealift transportation services to deploy, employ, and sustain US forces on a global basis. MSC executes this mission with the active fleet, to include prepositioned afloat assets, on a daily basis. MSC also assumes OPCON of additional shipping directed for acquisition by USTRANSCOM and DOD. This shipping consists of inactive assets. Inactive assets include US Navy owned and maintained ships kept in the ROS fleet and ships acquired and maintained by the MARAD. MSC also manages civilian chartered shipping and accessorial services when these support a military operation. Joint Pub 4-01.2 contains more information on the operations of MSC.

Military Traffic Management Command

2-21. MTMC is a major command of the US Army and the USTRANSCOM's surface transportation component of military traffic. MTMC's four core competencies are global traffic management, worldwide port operations, deployability engineering, and integrated transportation systems.

2-22. As a part of its programs to accomplish its wartime mission, MTMC administers the CORE program. This program consists of support agreements with the CONUS based commercial transportation industry. MTMC can activate this program to support emergency DOD transportation requirements before an official declaration of a national emergency.

2-23. DOD also tasks MTMC with the administration of national defense transportation programs. These programs assure the maintenance of an adequate US-based transportation infrastructure capable of responding rapidly to developing emergencies. Formal MTMC national defense transportation programs include highways, railroads, and ports. MTMC also administers transportability programs to ensure the incorporation of safe, efficient, and effective deployment characteristics into equipment design. MTMC conducts surveys of CONUS ports through the ports for National Defense Program and will conduct surveys of OCONUS ports in peacetime at the request of the CINC.

DEFENSE LOGISTICS AGENCY

2-24. The DLA provides supplies common to all military Services. The DTS recognizes DLA as a shipper. DLA coordinates with the supported CINC and Service components when the military operation requires the deployment of a DLA support team to the AO. DLA, through the DFSC, coordinates the movement of bulk fuels with the JPOs located within the J4 staff of the combatant commanders.

DEFENSE MAPPING AGENCY

2-25. The DMA provides mapping, charting, and geodesy support based on CINC requirements. The DMA produces standard maps; charts; map substitutes (for example, satellite image maps); and terrain data (elevation, slope, soils, vegetation, transportation infrastructure, hydrology, and so on). These are produced in hard copy (paper) and digitized (CD-ROM data tapes, and so on) formats for C2 systems and STAMIS (including DAMMS-R).

US SPACE COMMAND AND ARMY SPACE COMMAND

2-26. SPACECOMs provide satellite imagery and satellite communications support to both DMA and end users. They provide a contingency pool of INMARSAT terminals to users on a first-come, first-served basis. They also provide user training for space-based systems.

MILITARY POSTAL SERVICE AGENCY

2-27. Mail is one of the most important commodities moved during the conduct of a military operation. To assure the expeditious movement of mail, the MPSA has the following missions:

- Achieving efficient and economical transportation of official and personal mail throughout DOD.

- Establishing military postal offices in the AO.

- Maintaining operational command of subordinate JMPA.

2-28. JMPA are the main operating agencies in the mail delivery system. JMPA responsibilities include:

- Acting as the single point of contact with the USPS at the mail gateways.

- Coordinating the movement of mail with USTRANSCOM and the responsible movement control organization within the AO.

- Coordinating the transportation of mail to the AO to include transportation needs in the HN.

- Coordinating mail routing scheme changes with the mail gateways.

OTHER FEDERAL AGENCIES

2-29. Need lead in when this FM is updated.

FEDERAL EMERGENCY MANAGEMENT AGENCY

2-30. FEMA is responsible for coordinating federal responses to a domestic crisis. In this role, they orchestrate the support provided by DOD and other federal departments (Human and Health Services, Transportation, and so on) when disasters such as earthquakes and enemy attacks occur within the US. FEMA plays a key role in the management of CONUS transportation resources. However, this role is only visible to the US military when there is DOD involvement in response to a domestic emergency. FEMA also will be visible when the US is mounting a response to a foreign military crisis concurrent with a domestic crisis which results in a shortage of resources.

2-31. FEMA's most important transportation role is the maintenance of contingency plans to respond to crises arising from resource availability. Examples are, market disruptions, domestic transportation stoppages, and materiel shortages. FM 100-19 contains more information on the role FEMA plays during responses to crisis.

DEPARTMENT OF TRANSPORTATION

2-32. The DOT is responsible for the executive management of the nation's total civil domestic transportation resources during periods of crisis. The OET is the Secretary's peacetime staff element responsible for emergency transportation planning. The Secretary of Transportation sets up a management organization during a national defense related emergency declared by the President. By presidential direction, the Secretary of Transportation also implements control systems to govern the priority use of all civil transportation and the allocation of its capacity to meet essential civil and military needs. Federal transportation agencies carry out plans in consonance with overall policy direction of the Secretary of Transportation. Army transportation personnel, at staff and command levels, must communicate Army requirements for favorable adjudication. The DOT executes its emergency programs through several agencies. These agencies include the following:

The Federal Aviation Administration

2-33. The FAA is responsible for:

- Operating the national airspace systems and civil air/general aviation transportation facilities including air traffic control. The President has authority to transfer responsibility for some elements of air traffic control functions to DOD in time of war.

- Administering the WASP to maintain essential civil and air service during times of national emergency. Joint Pub 4-01.1 contains more information on the WASP program.

- Providing priority service orders to support DOD priority requirements.

- Administering the Title XIII insurance program for CRAF carriers.

The Federal Highway Administration

2-34. The FHWA administers movement on federal highways. One of its primary responsibilities is safety. The FHWA, in coordination with the state highway departments and organized users of highways, develops an emergency highway traffic regulation plan. This plan envisions, among other controls, the use of road space permits to control traffic over selected roads.

Maritime Administration

2-35. The MARAD administers programs related to ocean and Great Lakes shipping and related deep water activities including seaports, shipbuilding, and repair facilities. It also manages the RRF. This fleet is the most significant source of government-owned, early deployment shipping in terms of numbers of ships and overall cargo carrying capacity. The RRF is acquired and maintained by MARAD using funds appropriated to DOT from DOD for that purpose. USTRANSCOM, acting for DOD and with the approval of the SECDEF, requests the activation of RRF ships from MARAD. Upon activation, RRF ships operate under the USTRANSCOM combatant command and MSC operational control authorities.

2-36. MARAD is also responsible for acquiring and maintaining ships during emergencies. Section 902 of the Merchant Marine Act, 1936, as amended, contains the congressional authority for this action. Under these conditions, the MARAD accomplishes the following tasks:

- Establishing the National Shipping Authority as the executive agency for management of national shipping and port operations and, in a NATO contingency, as the national claimant upon the NATO shipping pool.

- Acquiring ocean shipping by:

- Requisitioning US-flag merchant ships, US-owned ships registered under foreign flags, and ships subject to requisition under the Emergency Foreign Vessels Acquisition Act of 1954.

- Coordinating with the NATO Defense Shipping Authority to get an allocation of European NATO-flag ships for service of the US.

- Chartering neutral ships, as available and required.

- Allocating shipping capacity to DOD jurisdiction and control and providing additional shipping capacity under MARAD conrol to meet DOD requirements.

- Recruiting and using manpower to meet requirements of ocean shipping and shoreside shipping-related operations.

2-37. In addition to the responsibilities listed above, MARAD sets up controls to balance the requirements levied on civil port capabilities by the military and private sector. MARAD also implements standby contractual arrangements for the priority use or allocation of selected ports for exclusive DOD use and for other federal uses. This responsibility includes arranging for the use of civil port facilities as auxiliary ammunition ports.

2-38. MARAD activates an emergency port control organization as part of the National Shipping Authority's emergency field organization. The emergency port control organization assures that local port industries provide situation reports through the National Shipping Authority to all interested agencies. Local MARAD port control officers coordinate with DOD authorities to assure the availability of commercial port capabilities to support military operations. This effort includes the employment of high-technology shipping systems.

US Coast Guard

2-39. The USCG is responsible for maritime and inland waterway security, port security, and safety including navigational aids. It establishes and certifies ammunition loading procedures and port capability within CONUS.

2-40. In peacetime, the DOT administers the USCG. Upon declaration of war, the USCG comes under OPCON of the Department of the Navy for port security and safety responsibilities. These responsibilities are for CONUS and OCONUS AO. USCG's role in licensing additional mariners to serve expanded defense shipping needs is integral to the mobilization process.

The Federal Railroad Administration

2-41. The FRA is responsible for the following functions:

- Consolidating government support of rail transportation activities.

- Providing unified national rail policy.

- Administering and enforcing rail safety laws and regulations.

- Administering financial assistance programs for selected railroads.

- Co-administering the railroads for the National Defense Program with USTRANSCOM.

- Conducting research and development in support of intercity ground transportation and future requirements for rail transportation.

- Providing federal overview of all "AMTRAK" passenger service.

St. Lawrence Seaway Development Corporation

2-42. This corporation is responsible for keeping the US-controlled sections of the St. Lawrence Seaway navigable.

Urban Mass Transportation Administration

2-43. This administration is responsible for aiding DOT in planning, financing, and developing urban mass transportation systems, facilities, and equipment.

THE DEPARTMENT OF ENERGY

2-44. The Department of Energy assures the availability of crude oil, petroleum products, solid fuels, natural gas, and gaseous liquids. Using its subordinate agency, the Federal Energy Regulatory Agency, the department also regulates the movement of these products through pipelines.

THE DEPARTMENT OF HEALTH AND HUMAN SERVICES

2-45. The Department of Health and Human Services has the responsibility for receiving, processing, and relocating noncombatant evacuees within the US.

THE DEPARTMENT OF STATE

2-46. The Department of State is responsible for several aspects that affect transportation operations. These aspects include the following:

- Negotiating HNS agreements.

- Operating the noncombatant evacuation program (except for DOD-sponsored personnel).

- Coordinating the delivery of humanitarian assistance in foreign areas. This coordination involves the participation of the OFDA. OFDA belongs to the Agency for International Development.

- Coordinating country clearance and overflight/transit clearances for forces, vessels, and aircraft entering or transiting a nation.

THE INTERSTATE COMMERCE COMMISSION

2-47. The ICC regulates interstate surface transportation services. These services include those provided by rail, freight and passenger motor carrier, inland waterways, coastal shipping, and freight forwarders. Before and during mobilization, the ICC, at the request of DOD and as approved by DOT, issues priority service orders to civil transportation carriers to support DOD priority requirements.

UNITED STATES POSTAL SERVICE

2-48. The USPS moves essential military mail, including small spare parts. The USPS also coordinates with the JMPAs located in the AO for the movement of mail through established gateways.

THE NATIONAL OCEANIC AND ATMOSPHERIC ADMINISTRATION

2-49. The National Oceanic and Atmospheric Administration provides aeronautical data and environmental weather services to DOD, as required.

STATE AND LOCAL TRANSPORTATION ORGANIZATIONS

2-50. Organizations responsible for transportation matters vary in size and responsibility from state to state. These organizations consist of those levels of government that have functional or modal responsibilities for water (including inland waterway), rail, motor carriers, or air transportation. In times of emergency, the main responsibility of these organizations is to coordinate personnel and cargo movements, to include convoys through the state highway system. During declared emergencies, the offices within the states operate under the general supervision and guidance of the regional offices established by the DOT.

2-51. During emergencies, the state and local governments are also responsible for using transportation resources transiting the state boundaries. Federal policies, issued by national control systems established by DOT and FEMA, govern the state and local governments responses. Under these circumstances, state and local governments comply with federal control measures to assure that interstate and international movements flow without interruptions.

CIVIL CARRIERS AND ASSOCIATIONS

2-52. Transportation carriers operate their facilities to provide maximum service, within their capabilities, to fulfill the requirements specified by appropriate government authorities. USTRANSCOM, through its component commands and programs such as CORE and CRAF, assure that these services include:

- Continuity of management.
- Protection of personnel and facilities.
- Conservation of supplies.
- Restoration of damaged lines and terminals.
- Security of personnel, material, and services.

SERVICE SECRETARIES

2-53. The Service Secretaries have single manager transportation responsibilities prescribed by Title 10, US Code. The Secretary of the Army is the single manager for land transportation, the Secretary of the Navy for sea transportation, and the Secretary of the Air Force for air transportation. The Service Secretaries discharge these responsibilities through the TCCs assigned to USTRANSCOM.

2-54. The Service Secretaries are also charged with the responsibility of providing CINCs with trained and equipped forces to execute assigned missions. This responsibility includes coordinating and resourcing the Army force for its movement to theater destination.

DEPARTMENT OF THE ARMY

2-55. Within the Army, the staff responsibility for transportation matters rests with the DCSOPS and the DCSLOG. Within DCSLOG, the principal staff element that coordinates the transportation effort is the Transportation, Energy, and Troop Support Directorate.

2-56. The Army Corps of Engineers also performs a transportation staff function. The Corps is responsible for the improvement, restoration, rehabilitation, operation, and maintenance of inland waterways, canals, harbors, and navigation channels within the US and its possessions. The exception to this role is the waterways associated with the TVA. The Department of Interior controls the TVA waterways. The Army Corps of Engineers executes these missions in time of crises under the policy direction of the Secretary of Transportation.

ARMY ORGANIZATIONS ASSIGNED TO COMBATANT COMMANDS

2-57. All combatant commands have an Army service component command. The Army service component command is the senior Army command directly subordinate to a combatant command. JTFs usually have an Army service component command. The Army service component command plans and executes the land warfare missions assigned to the combatant command or JTF. The plans cover the range of military operations.

2-58. Army execution of transportation functions differ based on the regional responsibilities of the combatant commands. Regional combatant commands based OCONUS have active Army transportation units assigned to deploy, receive, redeploy, and onward move personnel and equipment. Within CONUS, FORSCOM is the Army service component command for USACOM. FORSCOM uses Army installation staffs and infrastructures to deploy units and to receive and reconstitute a returning force.

THE ARMY SERVICE COMPONENT COMMANDER

2-59. The ASCC is responsible for advising the CINC on the transportation capabilities that the Army can bring to a joint operation. The advice includes the development of a theater-wide distribution system. It also includes advice on requirements for Army transportation units to provide a movement control terminal and mode operation capability in support of the system.

2-60. During the development of the distribution system, the ASCC considers the transportation support the command must give to other Services, as directed by the CINC. Depending on the size of the force deployed, the operational transportation responsibilities of the ASCC may also include tactical level responsibilities. The smaller the force, the more melding of functions will occur between operational and tactical level transportation operations. In the area of transportation, the ASCC is specifically responsible for the following:

- Developing the deployment plan for the Army units assigned to the command.

- Determining the size and type of transportation force structure.

- Establishing linkages between the operational and tactical levels of war transportation systems.

- Coordinating with the ITO or other supporting movement control organizations.

- Integrating Army transportation capability with other Service component assets.

- Acquiring HN transportation resources to increase Army capabilities.

- Recommending the sequence to deploy and receive Army transportation organizations. These recommendations include the following:

  ▪ Type of organizations needed to exercise the movement control functions delegated to the Army by the JFC.

  ▪ Type and number of transportation terminal operating units needed to support the distribution responsibilities assigned to the Army.

  ▪ Type and number of transportation mode operating units needed to support the distribution responsibilities assigned to the Army.

2-61. Depending on the size of the force deployed, the ASCC will have staff elements to assist in the accomplishment of its transportation responsibilities. The normal staff element at EAC is the DCSLOG TRANS. Based on the size of the force, the staff element may be a DTO or CTO. These staff elements are responsible for the following planning and execution functions:

- Advising the ASCC and staff on transportation matters, to include HNS.
- Providing technical assistance.
- Coordinating transportation staff actions.
- Conducting appropriate level of war planning.
- Evaluating transportation effectiveness.
- Publishing guidance for the preparation of the Army portion of the movement program.
- Coordinating the validation process for theater airlift.

2-62. The ASCC also acquires organizations to administer movements and to operate terminals and modes. Movement control organizations may consist of a TAMCA. This organization supports a force at EAC. The Corps and the Army division have organic movement control organizations and offices to execute this function. The Corps uses the MCC assigned to the Corps Support Command to execute the movement control functions. This center operates with organic MCTs, as required. At the division, the DTO, in coordination with the DISCOM MCO, performs the movement control functions.

2-63. The Corps or division movement control organizations execute tactical level of war transportation functions. They may require augmentation when executing operational level of war transportation responsibilities. Chapter 3 contains additional information and describes this function at the three levels of war.

2-64. The ASCC acquires terminal units to operate the transportation terminals. Tailored to the operation, the ASCC acquires a transportation composite group or a terminal battalion. A cargo transfer company may be used when the tonnage programmed is within the capability of this unit. HN or contracted support is a good source of resources to conduct or augment terminal operations. Chapter 4 contains additional information and describes this function at the three levels of war.

2-65. The ASCC organizes its transportation organizations with sufficient mode operators to move the programmed cargo. Mode operators are rail, truck, and medium helicopter companies. The ASCC may set up lighterage operations when inland waterways or an intra-coastal system are available in the AO. HN or contracted support is also a good source of resources to conduct or augment mode operations. Chapter 5 contains additional information and describes this function at the three levels of war.

ARMY MATERIEL COMMAND

2-66. The Army Materiel Command supports the Army in developing warfighting materiel and the ASCCs with a LSE. The Army Materiel Command may deploy a LSE into an AO to support the request of an ASCC. The team deploys using FORSCOM procedures. These procedures are described below.

CONUS BASED ARMY SERVICE COMPONENT COMMAND

2-67. FORSCOM commands and controls the deployment of CONUS based Army forces. Forward presence ASCC establish similar procedures to deploy forces in their AOR. The responsibilities are described below.

US Army Forces Command

2-68. FORSCOM, as the Army component of USACOM, has the primary responsibility within CONUS to provide the Army force projection or reinforcing forces required by a supported CINC. To accomplish this mission, FORSCOM, in coordination with the Army staff and USTRANSCOM, accomplishes the following tasks:

- Maintaining the DA master file of standard UMD to support the planning and operation requirement of the AMOPES and JOPES.

- Maintaining an automated interface with the GCCS for entrance into JOPES.

- Producing UMD for Army-type units for inclusion in the JOPES-type unit characteristics files used in JOPES.

- Functioning as the Army coordinating authority in support of deployment plans developed by combatant commands and as the initial operations focal point in performing deployments directed by the CINCs.

- Coordinating subordinate unit movement requirements for Army transportation support as allocated by USTRANSCOM. The transportation staff officers of the deploying units and the ITO participate in the coordination effort.

CONUS Installation Transportation Officer

2-69. Commanders of Army installations and garrisons, using the resources of their ITO TMO, are responsible for planning and executing the physical movement of tenant units. Specifically, the ITO executes the following tasks:

- Acting as the main point of contact for unit deployment transportation requirements.

- Helping unit personnel to develop and execute unit movement plans and documents.

- Coordinating with MTMC to acquire necessary transportation resources to support the deployment of units by all modes from home station/mobilization station to SPOEs or APOEs.

- Acting as the key interface between deploying units and DTS when using strategic transportation assets.

- Using the TC-ACCIS to provide deployment information into JOPES.

- Appointing an installation UMC. Unit movement officers will use the UMC as their primary linkage to the transportation support arranged for by the ITO. The UMC is normally in the ITO staff or assigned to the DOL, Plans and Operations Division. The installation UMC provides valuable movement information on the development of practical movement plans. The UMC will:

■ Serve as the central point of contact between deployable units, FORSCOM, and the USTRANSCOM TCCs for receipt and submission of UMD.

■ Assure that unit movement officers update their UMD and that it reflects current accurate data.

■ Approve unit movement plans, coordinate movement requirements, and maintain unit movement documents for movement by all applicable modes.

■ Maintain current data on the number and type of railcars or commercial trucks required to move units to the SPOE.

■ Assure the movement plan is compatible with installation capabilities.

■ Coordinate supercargo and rail guard requirements.

■ Coordinate requests for convoy clearances and special hauling permits, coordinate with state highway department, and ensure compliance with legal restrictions. This coordination may include contacts with the state DMCs.

■ Coordinate with unit and ITO for issue and receipt of military shipping containers.

■ Consult with representatives from the SPOE on vehicle reduction requirements that may be peculiar to constraints imposed by the ship stow plan.

■ Verify the AUEL data with units and submit changes to FORSCOM. During deployment execution, the UMC will submit changes to FORSCOM and MTMC.

■ Coordinate with the ITO to request the proper number and type of commercial transportation assets from commercial carriers. The UMC prepares the requests for commercial transport according to the routing instructions received from MTMC.

■ Monitor loading and unloading sites.

■ Notify the deploying commander of the SPOE/APOE loading schedule. Movement to the SPOE/APOE should coincide with the port call schedule provided by MTMC or AMC.

- Provide necessary support to mobilized USAR units for timely movement to mobilization stations (refer to AR 5-9).

- Report movement of units as directed (using TC-ACCIS ISR or command specified report).

- Help unit commanders coordinate with the installation Directorate of Public Works to identify blocking, bracing, packing, and crating materials in support of unit deployments.

- Monitor the status of containers and MILVANs in the installation area.

- Provide technical assistance in supporting unit deployment training.

- Provide assistance in the application of MSLs.

Continental Numbered Armies

2-70. FORSCOM's CONUSA provide support as directed.

State Area Commands

2-71. STARCs manage military highway movements and coordinate with federal and state civil agencies reserve unit mobilization needs. The DMCs, working within the SMCC, collects, analyzes, and combines all DOD-organic highway movements to coordinate with other local, state, and federal officials the unit requirements for mobilization and deployment. FM 100-17 contains information on the responsibilities of the STARCs.

Transportation Terminal Battalions or Brigades

2-72. The TTBs are RC TDA units. MTMC assumes command of the TTBs upon their mobilization. MTMC uses the TTBs to augment its terminal operating capability or to open new water terminals. The TTBs require the availability of contract stevedoring labor. MTMC selects a battalion or a brigade to operate a water terminal using the size of the operation as a primary determinant. When coordinated with USTRANSCOM, CINCs may use TTBs to support operations at force projection destinations.

Deployment Support Brigades

2-73. The DSBs are TDA RC units that when mobilized, operate under the command authority of MTMC. DSBs assist ITOs of installations with specific deployment activities. DSBs assist deploying units with documenting, staging, and loading their equipment. DSBs also provide liaison and coordination for movement of port-called units to designated terminals. DSBs do not perform actual loading operations. In addition to providing assistance on annual training missions, DSBs also provide technical assistance during scheduled individual training dates (mandatory unit training assembly). When coordinated with USTRANSCOM, CINCs may use DSBs to support operations at force projection destinations.

Other Activities

2-74. Other DOD and governmental agencies play a major role as users of the transportation system. Supported and supporting combatant commanders must consider their transportation requirements and assure that proper coordination is effected to accommodate their shipments. Among these organizations are AAFES and GSA.

Chapter 3

Army Movement Control

Need lead in when this FM is updated.

INTRODUCTION

3-1. Movement control is the planning, routing, scheduling, controlling, and coordinating responsibility for movements. Movement control also includes responsibility for ITV of personnel, units, equipment, and supplies moving over LOC. It includes the commitment of assigned modes and terminal assets according to command planning directives. Movement control exists at all levels of war and through the range of military operations. It is established regardless of the political nature of the US involvement. It is the most critical element of the Army transportation system.

SECTION I - Movement Control Principles and Functions

THE PRINCIPLES OF MOVEMENT CONTROL

3-2. Five principles govern the planning and execution of movement control operations. These principles are as follows:

- Centralized Control/Decentralized Execution.
- Regulated Movements.
- Fluid and Flexible Movement.
- Maximum Use of Carrying Capacity.
- Forward Support.

Figure 3-1, page 3-1, portrays the importance of these principles.

CENTRALIZED CONTROL/DECENTRALIZED EXECUTION

3-3. The most efficient method to provide movement control is to centralize control of movements at the highest level. Centralization means that a focal point for transportation planning and resource allocation must exist at each level of command involved in an operation. The focal point is an individual or unit that is aware of the current and future requirements of the supported force as well as the capabilities available to meet the requirements. Centralization of movement control normally occurs at the levels charged with integrating logistic support. Decentralized control of mode and terminal operations are equally important. Decentralized execution of transportation missions means terminal and mode operators remain free to assign and control the specific transportation asset that will meet the requirement. This practice enhances the flexibility to prioritize support and accomplish the mission.

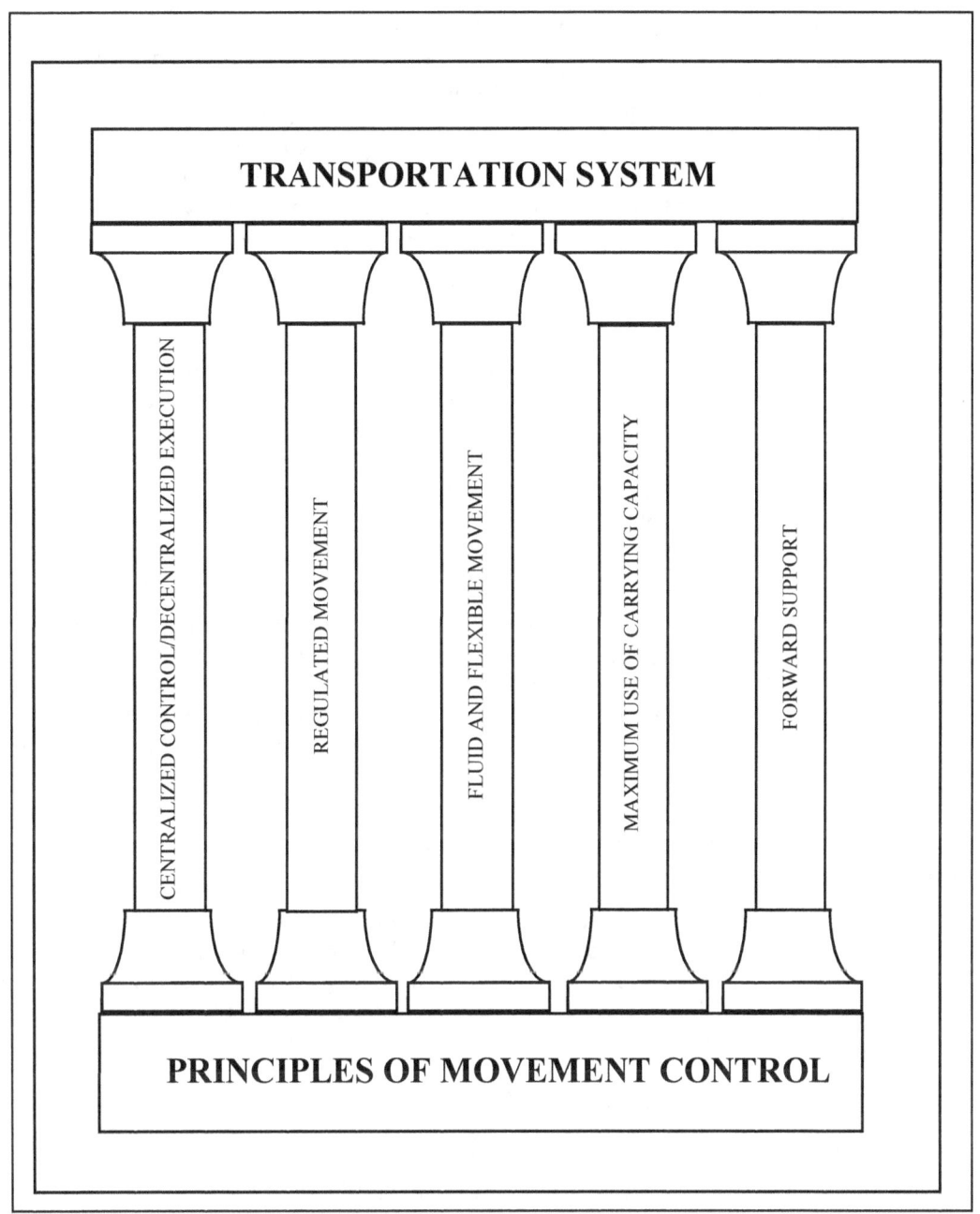

Figure 3-1. Movement Control Principles

REGULATED MOVEMENTS

3-4. The regulation of movements has two applications. One deals with the apportionment of cargo carrying capacities to movement requirements. The second deals with the regulation of traffic through the LOC, including MSRs.

3-5. Transportation planners must determine which traffic and LOC requires control. The free flow of goods and services will work in a nonsaturated environment. However, saturation of the system normally occurs because highly mobile forces extend resupply lines. Increased consumption rates and a desire to reduce stockpiles are additional causes of saturation of the transportation system. Inadequate transportation capabilities in relationship to the size of the force supported will also require astute prioritization efforts.

3-6. An additional consideration is the support the Army provides to the other Services. In a joint and combined environment, regulation of transportation assets and LOC will prevent congestion and enforce priorities. Regulation of LOC movements are critical. This is always important when US forces must share available airfields, roads, rail lines, water terminals, and inland waterways with allied forces and the HN. A clear articulation of priorities is essential. MP organizations help by providing security, reconnaissance, and traffic control.

3-7. Command priorities guide the regulation of all movements. In this regard, transportation planners, operators, and users must exercise discipline when establishing and using available transportation assets. The exercise of discipline assures meeting the commander's priorities. A disciplined transportation system enhances the confidence users have in the system's ability to support the mission. When planning and executing movements, commanders must not validate, approve, or start any move if a terminal or mode in the transportation system cannot meet the requirement.

FLUID AND FLEXIBLE MOVEMENT

3-8. The transportation system must provide for the uninterrupted flow of traffic. This means the system must be capable of rerouting and diverting traffic. Maintaining flexibility is one of the biggest challenges facing transportation planners and operators in a changing battlefield with shifting conditions and priorities. To accomplish this task successfully, the transportation system must be linked to an information and communications system. These systems provide data in time to adjust the responses of the terminals and modes in the system. AITs are an essential component in providing timely data. For more information on AIT see Appendix A.

3-9. Transportation planners and operators can also improve response time and flexibility by using the right modes for the right cargo. They can also anticipate the need for alternate modes and routes.

MAXIMUM USE OF CARRYING CAPACITY

3-10. This principle involves more than loading each transport vehicle to its maximum carrying capacity. It also means using all available transport capability in the most efficient manner. While allowing for adequate equipment maintenance and personnel rest, transportation operators should keep transportation assets loaded and moving as much as the operational and tactical situation permits.

3-11. The discipline of the transportation system also plays an important role in the execution of this principle. Transport vehicles and containers need fast off-loading and return to the system to increase the transport capability for later operations.

3-12. Discipline in the prompt return of transportation assets assures their availability for subsequent operations and avoids possible demurrage, storage, and other penalty charges against the government. Similarly, transportation assets must support the retrograde of personnel and cargo operations.

FORWARD SUPPORT

3-13. The principle of forward support includes fast, reliable transportation to provide support as far forward as possible. Forward-oriented transportation support is a combat multiplier; it allows the commander to concentrate all his forces on the enemy. The key to forward support is the reception and clearance capabilities at the destination units. These units may require equipment and personnel augmentation to enhance their reception and clearance capabilities. Forward support may entail the provisioning of operational level transportation assets to support tactical level units. However, any requirement for forward support that relinquishes centralized control for an extended time must be balanced against the efficiency of the transportation system to provide time utility and to weigh the battle at decisive times and places.

OTHER CONSIDERATIONS

3-14. Need lead in when this FM is updated.

Peace to War

3-15. To the maximum extent possible, commanders assign transportation responsibilities, establish procedures, and train, using the same organizations throughout the range of military operations. From a movement control perspective, the initiation of a military operation should only represent an increase in intensity, not a shift to new procedures and systems.

3-16. Executing this consideration is not as simple as it may seem. For example, the force projection Army requires that CONUS based and forward presence transportation organizations become involved concurrently in both the strategic deployment of its organic elements and the planning of the transportation system needed to support the operation. An important factor is identifying and sequencing transportation elements during the deployment. This is crucial to the success of the operation. These elements must arrive in the AO at the right time and with the right equipment to get the transportation system functional.

3-17. The movement control elements should be among the early units deployed in the theater opening force modules. Early deployment will allow for the timely establishment of a transportation system with the capability to receive and program the onward movement of the deploying force and manage its growth.

During Desert Shield, despite the overwhelming demand for combat troops to defend Saudi Arabia, the initial force included a contingent from the 403d Transportation Company (Cargo Transfer) at Fort Bragg. This contingent managed the military operations at the airfield at Dhahran, illustrating the importance of deploying supporting transportation units prior to the supported force.

Origin to Destination

3-18. The goal of the Army transportation system is the movement of passengers and cargo from origin to destination. This goal can be achieved efficiently when the cargo and personnel do not have to be handled or processed frequently while in-transit. This concept of operations is called throughput. In addition to throughput, Army transportation organizations consider the intermodal capabilities available. Intermodality facilitates the handling of cargo while in-transit. To the maximum extent possible, Army transportation planners should strive to move cargo and personnel from origin to destination using throughput and intermodality as key considerations.

Port Opening Force Modules

3-19. The capabilities to operate water terminals in AO, to include the use of preposition afloat assets, will vary. This capability can be determined when planners consider the following:

- The mission of the force within the range of military operations.
- The political nature of the US involvement.

- The size of the deploying force.

- The capabilities of the facilities available within the AO.

To assist planners in designing port opening force modules, FM 100-17-1, Annex B, contains four modules that can be used as guides to develop the required port opening force.

Total Asset Visibility and In-transit Visibility

3-20. The TAV concept consists of two subordinate parts (asset visibility and in-transit visibility). Asset visibility covers resources in inventory, or static to the visibility system, and in-transit visibility which, as the name implies, covers resources in motion throughout the strategic, operational, and tactical continuums. The TAV concept has been translated into a computer software system which can track resources throughout the world. The software supports the battlefield distribution requirement to be able to identify, cross level, ship, or redirect assets to provide immediate support to the combatant. Additional information on TAV and communications support is contained in Appendix A.

THE FUNCTIONS OF MOVEMENT CONTROL

3-21. Joint Pub 4.01-3 describes six functions common to movement control activities regardless of the level of war at which they operate. Movement control is the planning, routing, scheduling, controlling, coordination, and ITV of personnel, units, equipment, and supplies moving over LOC and the commitment of allocated transportation assets according to the command planning directives. It is a continuum that involves synchronizing and integrating logistics, movement information, and programs that span the strategic, operational, and tactical levels of war. Movement control is guided by a system that balances requirements against capabilities and assigns resources based on the combat commanders priorities. Effective movement control is the linchpin that integrates logistics systems that sustain forces on the battlefield. As such, it becomes a combat multiplier. Army movement control encompasses these functions and provides staff planners and movement managers at each echelon to perform them. Staff planners plan and apportion. Movement managers allocate, coordinate, deconflict, and provide ITV (see Figure 3-2, page 3-6).

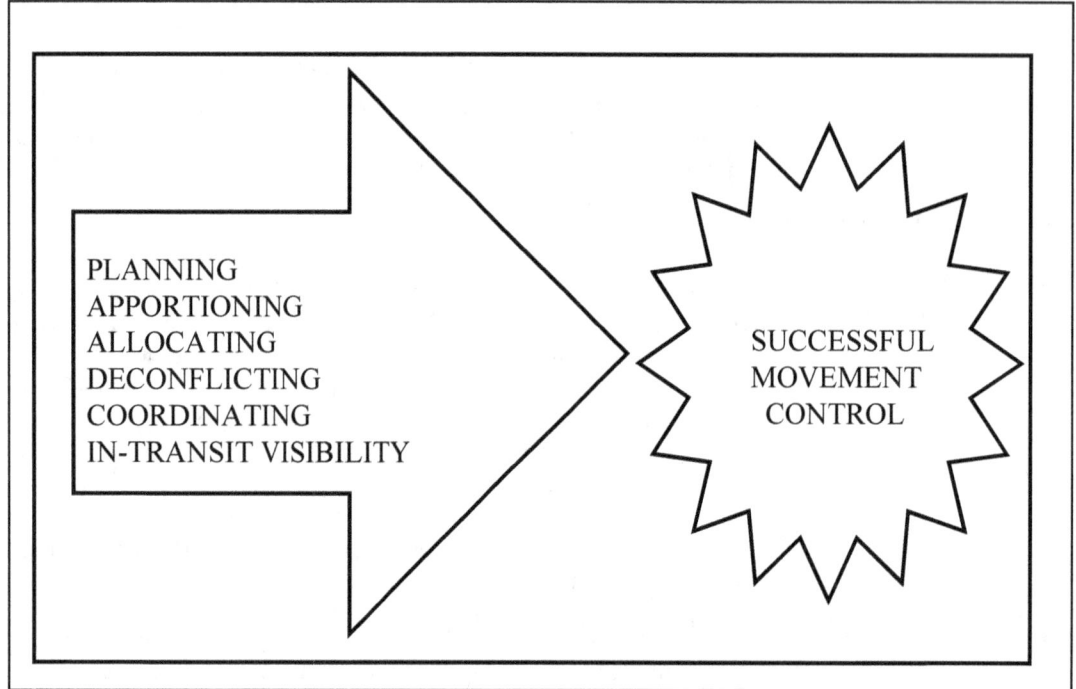

Figure 3-2. Movement Control Functions

STAFF PLANNING

3-22. Transportation planning is vital to the success of military operations at all levels of command. Staff planners serve on the coordinating or special staffs at each echelon of command. They perform common functions integral to deploying and sustaining the force. They provide expertise in the development of operation plans and estimates during the planning process. They also advise commanders and staff on transportation matters, coordinate transportation staff actions, and evaluate the effectiveness of the transportation system. Staff planners also coordinate with other functional planners that have an impact on transportation to ensure requirements which relate to the transportation system are adequately covered. Planners must look forward, backward, and laterally, as appropriate, to ensure plans are synchronized with supporting and supported commands. Figure 3-3, shows how movement control interfaces with all movement requirements.

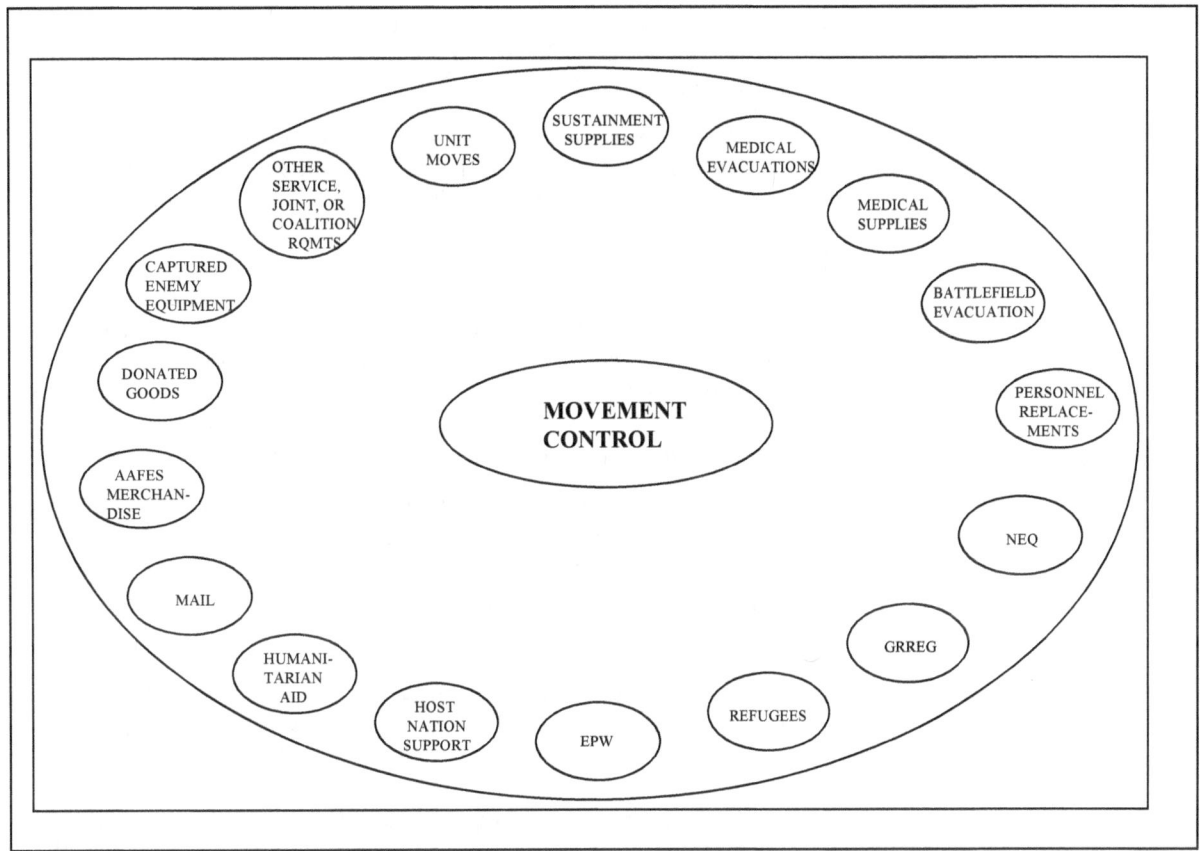

Figure 3-3. Movement Control Interface

Planning

3-23. At the strategic level, staff planners use strategic level systems, including JOPES, GTN, and TC-ACCIS, to plan the deployment and sustainment of forces during both deliberate planning and CAP. During CAP, planners work closely with other staff elements to convert the commander's concept of operations into a viable and transportation supportable OPORD and TPFDD. The window of opportunity for making decisions in this critical period is often very compressed. Decisions made during this period are often irretrievable, or at least very hard to change.

In operation RESTORE HOPE, the ARFOR window of opportunity effectively began with the publishing of the JTF deployment OPLAN on December 6, 1992. Preliminary conceptual planning had begun with receipt of the warning order on December 1; however, it contained little of the critical information required for detailed planning. The ARFOR's window ended on December 7, when the 10th Mountain Division began staging equipment for movement to the SPOE.

3-24. Equally important is coordination with the operational level to ensure a smooth transition between the strategic and operational transportation systems.

3-25. At the operational level, staff planners on the ASCC staff, plan support to the Army force from reception in the AO through movement to final destination. They have a dual responsibility. The ASCC contributes to the strategic transportation plan for deployment of forces and develops an operational level of war transportation plan. This plan ensures the ASCC has the capability for receiving, moving, and sustaining the force. The plan involves the selection of terminals and the number, type, and sequencing of transportation units needed in the theater. The ASCC continues its planning for expansion of the transportation system capability to support the total force projected for deployment.

3-26. Planning at the tactical level of war is just as critical. Tactical level transportation forms the structure of the final distribution system. It must be the most flexible and responsive to changing conditions. When completely fielded, DAMMS-R meets this need. The ability to divert and reroute based on changes in priorities, concepts of support, or DS to combat operations is paramount. Planners must consider the linkage to the operational level transportation system when selecting the location of their units.

Apportioning

3-27. Apportioning involves dividing the common-user transportation capability among the transportation tasks according to priorities. It is a critical function in decision making because it forces planners to analyze all transportation tasks and in the broad sense, divide the transportation capabilities among those tasks. At the strategic level, the CJCS apportions strategic lift assets during OPLAN development. Theater level apportionments support the CINC's concept of operations. They are usually expressed in percentages and developed in planning cycles. After receiving its share from the supported CINC, the ASCC apportions and distributes resources to the Army force. If the Army provides support to other services, then its apportionment of common-user lift must reflect that mission. Similar decisions are made at the operational and tactical level.

MOVEMENT MANAGEMENT

3-28. Movement management is the coordination of transportation support between transportation users and providers. It is performed by movement control units or staffs normally assigned to supporting commands, agencies, installations, and multifunctional logistical commands. Deployed, they are assigned to the ASCC, Corps, and divisions and include the TAMCA, MCC, and MCO.

3-29. Like staff planners, movement managers perform common functions that contribute to providing effective transportation support to the force. They are focused on allocating resources, coordinating support, deconflicting requirements, and providing ITV of movements.

3-30. Movement managers are the customer point of contact for transportation support and their point of entrance to the transportation system. They concentrate their efforts on those functions of movement control which directly relate to providing continuous transportation support. Their efforts are central and integral to effective transportation support by all modes.

3-31. They also conduct planning associated with these functions, mainly as supporting plans which focus on their areas of responsibility. Two functions which have broad planning application are movement programming and highway regulation. Movement managers also coordinate with all users of transportation, including material managers, to forecast requirements and plan appropriate support based on priorities. They work routinely with engineer and MP units that support the transportation system.

Allocating

3-32. Allocating is the assignment of specific transportation resources against planned movement requirements. The CINCs, through their JMC, usually delegate the allocation process to the Service components for the modes and terminals they operate. The Service components normally express allocations either by gross tonnages, number of vehicles, berthing time, number of aircraft, or other appropriate terms. These allocations are published in movement programs.

Coordinating

3-33. Coordinating is the process by which movement control units interface with units and shippers to provide transportation support. During this process, they match requirements with modes based on priorities and consider the principles of movement and mode selection criteria. Movement control units then commit or task mode and terminal operators to provide support. Coordination extends to allied forces, HNS, and non-governmental agencies within their AOR. Reliable communications enhances response time and are crucial to this process. A standard transportation request process and validation system are inherent to coordination.

Deconflicting

3-34. Movement managers deconflict requirements and priorities when there are not enough assets to satisfy all transportation requests. They also deconflict movement on LOC to prevent conflict and congestion. For movement on roads, this is referred to as highway regulation. To deconflict requirements, movement control units require automated support to receive transportation requests and movement bids, process them, and communicate schedules and itineraries to the requestor.

In-transit Visibility

3-35. ITV the continuous updating of the location of unit equipment, personnel, and supplies as they travel within the transportation system. It enables movement control units to answer the commander's information needs, divert shipments based on changes of priority or destination, and coordinate and deconflict movements. ITV is required at all levels of war. USTRANSCOM uses GTN and JOPES for strategic movements. Theater systems must provide similar capabilities and link with strategic systems. Assured communications are essential.

SECTION II - Movement Control at the Strategic Level of War

INTRODUCTION

3-36. Movement control at the strategic level of war is primarily the responsibility of DOD. This responsibility is shared by the combatant commands and the Services, with the support of non-DOD agencies and the private sector. The movement control focus is on the following:

- Force Projection.
- Sustaining the Forward Deployed Force.
- Strategic Mobility.

3-37. The creation and participation of movement control units throughout DTS accomplish the tasks. The apex of the system consists of USTRANSCOM, the supported and supporting CINCs JMC, and the Service components.

STRATEGIC MOVEMENT CONTROL IN PEACETIME

3-38. Strategic movement control in peacetime supports the combatant commands and the Services through DTS. The transportation system operates with the users of the system providing movement requirements to USTRANSCOM and its component commands. USTRANSCOM schedules the movement based on the transportation priorities. Consultation among USTRANSCOM, the Services, and mode operators resolves most conflicts. The process rarely requires the involvement of the Joint Staff JTB.

3-39. Army elements desiring transportation support enter the system through the ITO, movement control units, and transportation or movement managers found in other Army activities, such as depots. These elements receive movement requirements, act on those for which they have authority, and pass those that exceed their capabilities to the proper supporting organization. For example, CONUS ITOs pass requirements to MTMC, while forward presence units pass requirements to higher level movement control units. Each requirement receives a priority, movement is scheduled, and the participants informed of pick-up and delivery times, supporting assets, and cost.

3-40. Some shipments will require clearance from other agencies. These clearances include those that are granted by state highway regulators or HN authorities.

3-41. USTRANSCOM develops manifests and sends shipping information to receiving terminal and other interested parties. Using the GTN, USTRANSCOM provides shipping information to all users of DTS. Appendix A provides additional information on the GTN.

STRATEGIC MOVEMENT CONTROL IN SUPPORT OF MILITARY OPERATIONS

3-42. The decision to commit military forces implies strategic deployment of forces from CONUS. However, forward deployed forces may also have to move. Strategic deployments normally reinforce a joint operation or require a joint force projection. The Army's role is to support the deployment according to the requirements of the supported CINC. The Army uses its peacetime network of movement control organizations, terminals, and modes. This network is the building block to develop a movement control organization capable of supporting the deployment.

PLANNING FOR STRATEGIC MOVEMENT CONTROL

3-43. Need lead in when this FM is updated.

PLANNING METHODS

3-44. DOD strategic planning consists of deliberate planning and CAP. Deliberate planning is the method used when time permits the total participation of the commanders and staffs of the JPEC (see Figure 3-4, page 3-12). The JPEC consists of commands and agencies involved in the training, preparation, and movement of forces.

3-45. During peacetime, combatant commanders and their Service components use the deliberate planning process to develop CONPLANs and detailed OPLANs for contingencies identified in the JSCP. Development of these plans include coordination among supported and supporting commanders, agencies, and the Services. The Joint Staff, in conference with JPEC members, review the plans. This process can take many months.

3-46. CAP is the method used to respond militarily to emergency conditions in support of US interests. CAP occurs in response to specific situations as they occur. It may involve the revision of an existing plan or the creation of a new one. These situations normally develop rapidly.

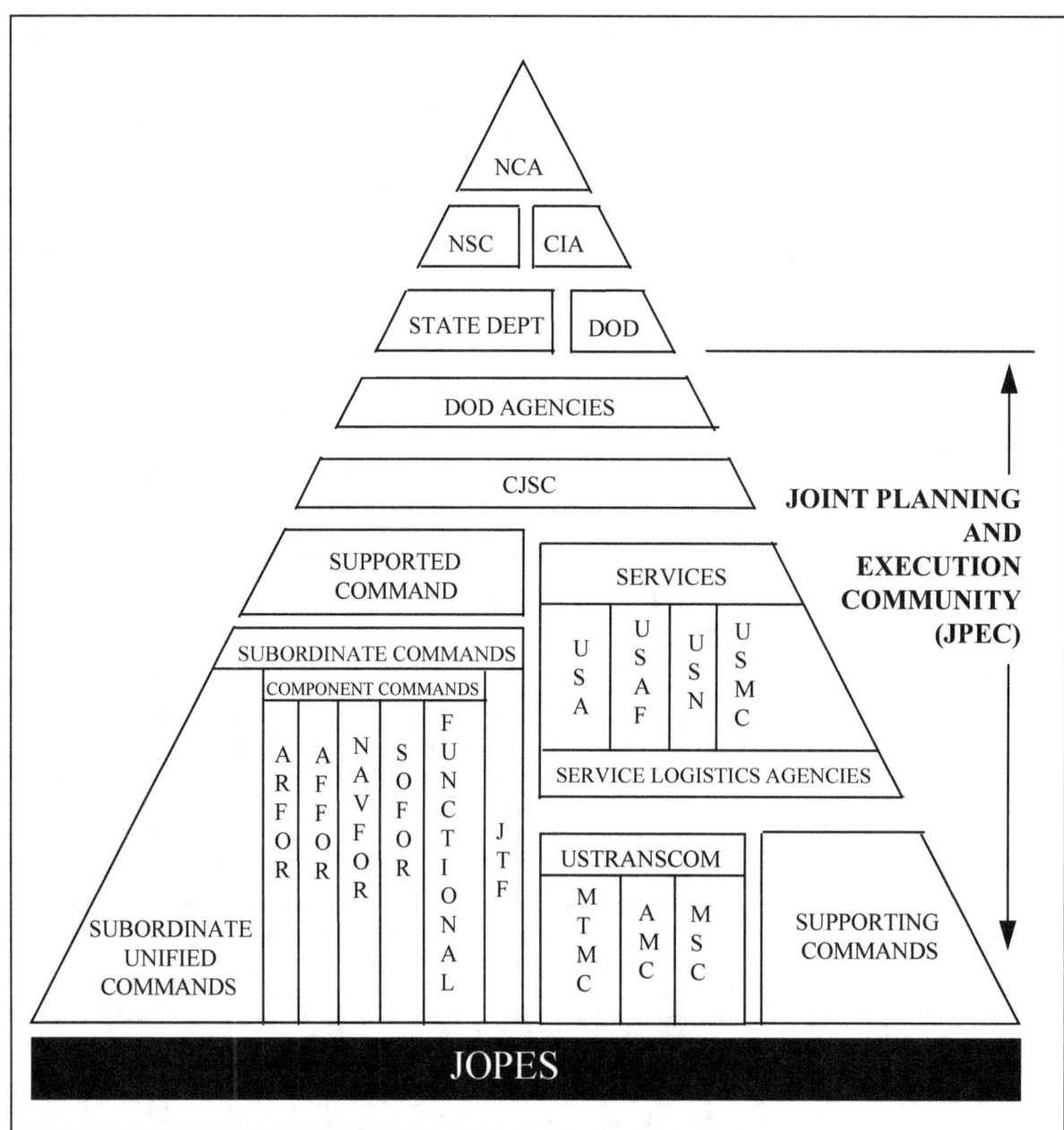

Figure 3-4. Players in the Deliberate Planning Process

3-47. During deliberate planning, combatant commanders also do adaptive planning. It is a concept that calls for the development of a range of options, encompassing the elements of national power (diplomatic, political, economic, and military) that can be adapted to a crisis as it develops. These options are referred to as the Flexible Deterrent Options. The adaptive planning concept recognizes that the US faces diversified threats and regional conflicts. Therefore, the fixed assumptions, warning times, and political decisions used in deliberate planning will be less accurate than those predicted by planners. As such, adaptive planning recognizes that key decision makers are more likely to exploit available response time to deter the development or deterioration of a crisis. This is possible if a menu of response options, gauged to a range of crisis conditions, is available for them to execute. The concept prevents an all or nothing choice.

INPUT TO PLANNING

3-48. Several key documents aid planning for strategic mobility and strategic movement control. Embedded in these documents are guidance on issues and funding which can have an impact on the military capability to deploy and sustain the force. The primary users of these documents are the Joint Staff, the combatant commands, and the Military departments. Figure 3-5, page 3-14, portrays the relationships.

National Military Strategy

3-49. The National Military Strategy furnishes the advice of the CJCS, in consultation with other members of the JCS and the combatant commanders, to the President, the NSC, and the SECDEF. The advice includes recommendations affecting the national military strategy and the fiscally constrained force structure required to support the attainment of national security goals. The national military strategy assists the SECDEF in preparing the DPG.

The Defense Planning Guidance

3-50. The DPG is a document issued by the SECDEF to the military departments. The DPG assists in the development of the military departments' POMs. The defense planning period comes from the POM. The DPG includes force and resource guidance, decisions, strategy, and policy. The DPG includes strategic elements, the Secretary's program planning goals, and the Defense Planning Estimate. The Illustrative Planning Scenarios and a whole series of studies are also included in the DPG.

Chairman's Guidance

3-51. The Chairman's Guidance conveys guidance to the Joint Staff and information to the SECDEF and combatant commanders about the framework for building the national military strategy and for setting priorities in the JPD.

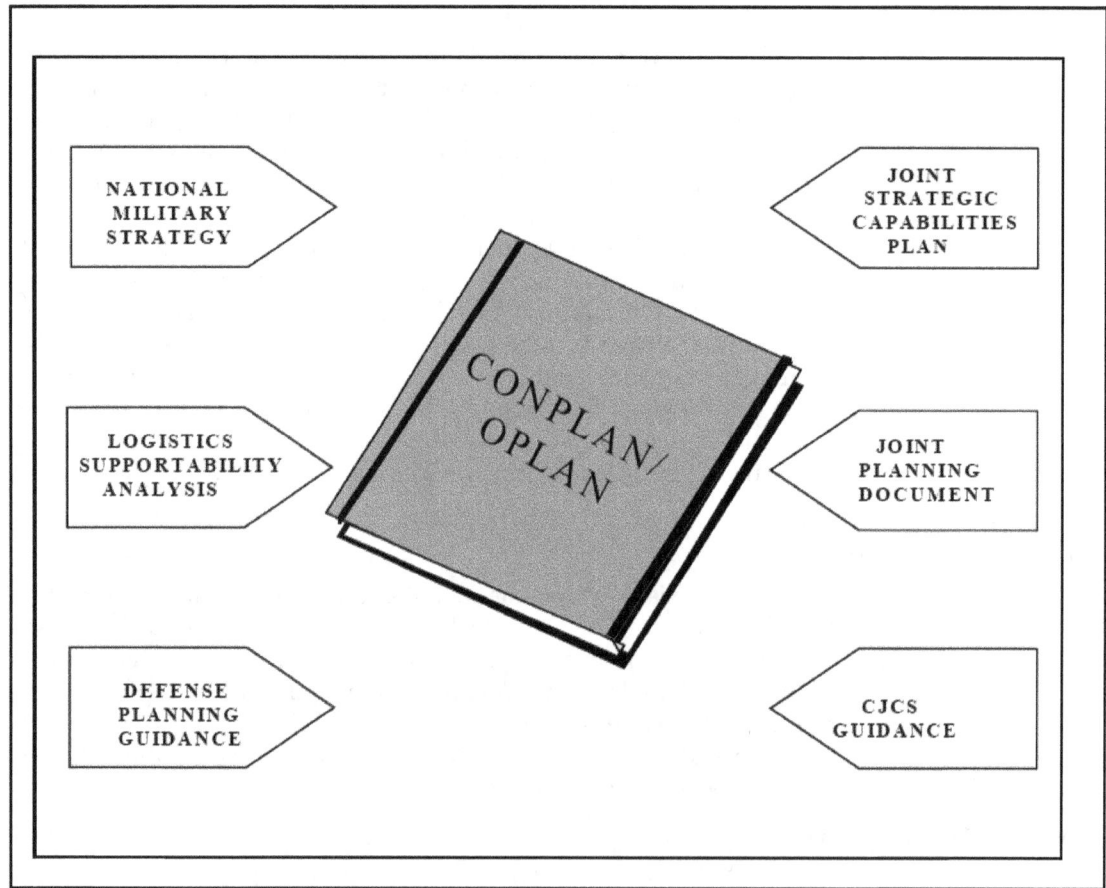

Figure 3-5. Input to Planning

Joint Planning Document

> 3-52. The JPD supports the national military strategy by furnishing concise programming priorities, requirements, or advice to the SECDEF for consideration during preparation of the DPG. The JPD is a series of volumes covering specific functional areas, including, Volume 7, "Logistics (J-4 Lead)," describing the joint logistics policies and programs that affect the capability of programmed forces to meet their present and future requirements.

Joint Strategic Capabilities Plan

3-53. The JSCP contains guidance to the CINCs and Service Chiefs for accomplishing military tasks and missions based on current military capabilities. It directs the development of contingency plans to support national security goals by assigning planning tasks and apportioning major combat forces and strategic lift capability to the combatant commanders. In short, it provides CINCs and the Service component commanders available resources to develop their contingency plans. The sixteen JSCP annexes furnish planning guidance and capabilities. Annex B, "Logistics," and Annex J, "Mobility," contain information applicable to transportation planners.

Logistics Sustainability Analysis

3-54. The LSA represents the quantitative assessment of the CINC's overall sustainment posture. The logistics capabilities and specific limiting factors associated with each OPLAN come from the LSA.

PLANNING SYSTEMS

3-55. JOPES is a DOD directed system of policies, procedures, and ADP support used in developing, maintaining, and executing OPORDs and OPLANs. JOPES is also a command and control system designed primarily to satisfy the information needs of senior-level decision makers. JOPES monitors, plans, and executes mobilization, deployment, employment, sustainment, and redeployment activities.

3-56. One of the key capabilities of JOPES is the development of transportation feasibility analysis and plans. The transportation feasibility analysis occurs after the CINC, supporting CINCs, and Service components develop TPFDD. The TPFDD is the supported CINC's statement of his requirements by unit type, time, and priority for arrival. The TPFDD also defines the supported CINC's nonunit-related cargo and personnel requirements and movement data for the OPLAN, including the following:

- In-place units.
- Deployable units to support the OPLAN with a priority that shows the supported CINC's sequence for their arrival at the POD.
- Deployed forces routing.
- Movement data associated with deploying forces.
- Estimate of nonunit-related cargo and personnel (fillers and replacements) movements conducted concurrently with the deployable unit.
- Estimate of transportation requirements fulfilled by common-user lift resources as well as those requirements fulfilled by assigned or attached transportation resources.

3-57. The TPFDD undergoes a refinement process during the plan development phase. This process considers any shortfall in forces, logistics, and transportation. The supported CINC is the decision making authority during this process unless otherwise directed by the CJCS. The purpose of the TPFDD refinement process is to adjust the proposed flow of the TPFDD assuring it is transportation-feasible and consistent with JSCP, Joint Staff, and Service guidance.

3-58. USCINCTRANS conducts TPFDD refinement conferences in coordination with the supported CINC, Joint Staff, Services, and supporting CINCs. During the conferences, participants address transportation related problems. They also coordinate combined transportation requirements and resolve shortfalls. Movement tables help the supported CINC determine whether the force closure profile is consistent with his concept of operations.

EXECUTION OF THE DEPLOYMENT

3-59. Once the deployment begins, necessary TPFDL adjustments will occur. These adjustments cause turbulence within the flow of the deployment. The turbulence occurs, especially in the early stages, because the CINC and the Service components must adjust their response to the threat and other factors influencing the flow of the force into the operational area. Figure 3-6, shows a notional representation of the turbulence normally experienced during deployments, especially in the early stages.

3-60. Commanders execute deployments within a very intense process influenced by the turbulence described above. The goal is to manage the turbulence through anticipation. Commanders must exercise discipline and ensure timely and accurate communications to facilitate the process. Transportation discipline can not occur unless each participant sets up a precise system to communicate information. Accurate communications results when each player exercises quality control over the information placed into the system. The players use data processing systems to the maximum extent possible. Other systems, such as telephones, are only used as required. Movement control plays a key role in this process by providing advice and assistance. Table 3-1, page 3-18, shows minimum connectivity requirements to assure the efficient use of resources in meeting the requirements of the commander.

STRATEGIC DEPLOYMENT PHASES

3-61. There are three strategic level phases of Army deployment activities. They consist of the following:

- Predeployment Activities.
- Movement to the POE.
- Strategic Lift.

3-61. Movement control plays a key role in each phase. The operational level phases, theater reception, and onward movement, are covered in Section III.

3-62. Army movement control differs for strategic deployments, depending on whether the force is CONUS or OCONUS based. Within CONUS, the ITO plays the key role in the execution of movement control activities to deploy the force. The movement control organization assigned to the deploying force supports the ITO. OCONUS based forces usually rely on their organic, deployable movement control units.

3-63. Deployable movement control units selected to support OPLANs have a dual responsibility during peacetime operations. They train to support the deployment of the force and prepare to participate in the deployment themselves. The deployment phasing must balance the need to support the deploying force with the need to establish the theater movement control system.

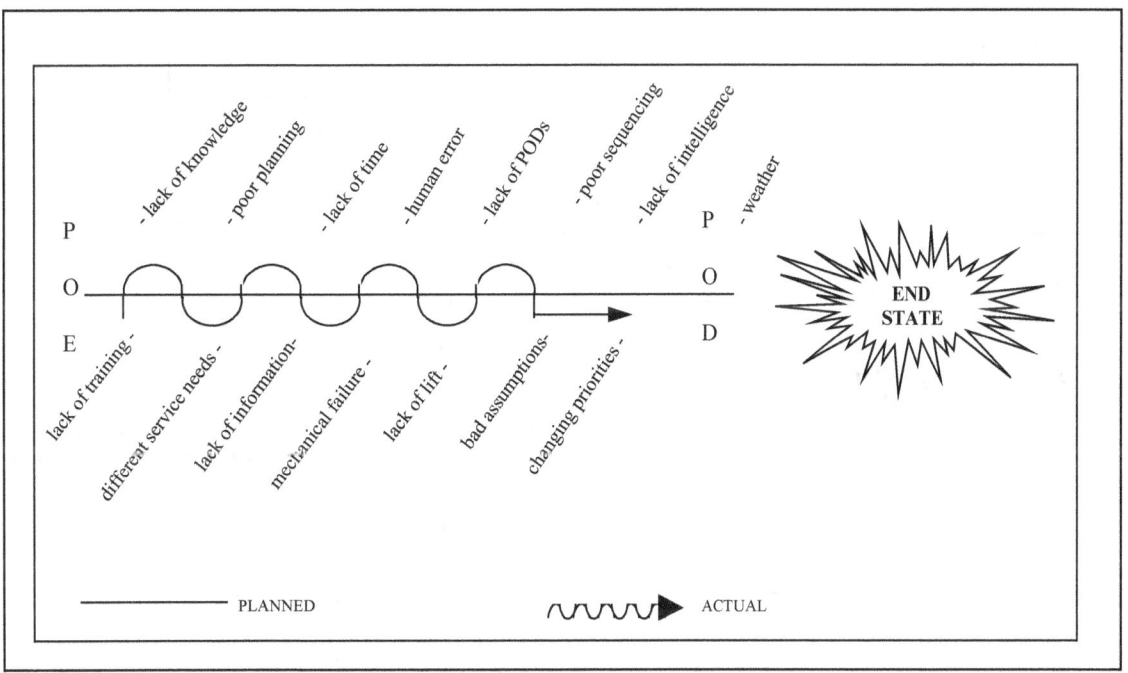

Figure 3-6. Turbulence During Deployments

Table 3-1. Deployment Information Exchange Connectivity

	JOINT STAFF	SUPPORTED CINC	SUPPORTING CINC	USTRANSCOM	AMC	MTMC	MSC	ASCC	DA STAFF	INSTALLATIONS	DEPLOYING UNITS
JOINT STAFF		X	X	X					X		
SUPPORTED CINC	X		X	X				X			
SUPPORTING CINC	X	X		X				X			
USTRANSCOM	X	X	X		X	X	X		X		
AMC				X				X			X
MTMC				X	X			X	X	X	
MSC				X		X		X		X	
ASCC		X	X		X	X	X		X	X	X
DA STAFF	X			X		X		X		X	
INSTALLATIONS					X	X	X	X	X		X
DEPLOYING UNITS								X		X	

PHASE 1 - PREDEPLOYMENT ACTIVITIES

3-64. Force projection missions are the focus of Army predeployment activities. Units conduct emergency deployment training to assure the Army can deploy the required forces, individual manpower, and materiel to meet the CINC's missions. Emergency deployment training includes the use of strategic airlift and sealift assets.

3-65. During emergency deployment exercises, commanders revise and update their movement plans. Army organizations responsible for providing sustainment also conduct exercises to test the movement of prepackaged supplies as required by the appropriate contingency plans. Commanders use the knowledge from the exercises to update deployment data such as the AUEL or TPFDD. These updated lists pass through the chain of command to the proper authority.

3-66. Commanders must decide what mission they will assign to their organic movement control organization during the execution of an actual deployment. Although these organizations participate in the planning and training functions exercised before a deployment, the commander reassesses the mission these organizations are to execute in the AO. If a nondeployable movement control organization is available and capable of supporting the deployment, commanders should consider not using the deployable movement control organization. If the deployment is large (division or higher), the commander may consider the echelonment of the deployable movement control organization.

3-67. Once the NCA directs a military response requiring a deployment, identified units (to include mobilized reserve components) coordinate with the responsible movement control organization for the execution of the deployment. The commander directs the flow of deployment orders to the movement control organizations. The supporting ASCC will coordinate with the supported command, USTRANSCOM, and its components, to assure the correct flow of the deployment orders.

3-68. Movement control units focus on coordinating transportation support, providing containers and pallets, synchronizing, staging, and marshaling operations with the deployment flow, and ensuring the accuracy of movement data. They advise the commander on all transportation aspects of the deployment.

PHASE 2 - MOVEMENT TO THE PORT OF EMBARKATION

3-69. This phase begins when Army units move to water or air terminals for embarkation to a force projection destination. The supported CINC, in coordination with the ASCC, USTRANSCOM, supporting CINCs, subordinate HQ, and the responsible movement control organization, orchestrates the movement. The CINC uses the refined TPFDL and unit readiness information provided to JOPES. USTRANSCOM, in coordination with the ASCC, provides movement guidance for movement to the POE based on the priorities established by the CINC. The information usually flows through the USTRANSCOM components to the responsible movement control organization. MTMC or the proper movement control organization specifies, by port call message, when unit equipment must be at the SPOE for loading into strategic lift. Based on the movement directive, units backward plan their installation departure and POE processing to meet their available load date.

3-70. The AMC specifies, through an air tasking order, when unit equipment and personnel need to arrive at the APOE for aircraft loading.

3-71. Movement control units focus on providing transportation support, obtaining movement clearances, and coordinating surface and air movements to the prescribed POE.

PHASE 3 - STRATEGIC LIFT

3-72. This phase begins with strategic lift departure from the POE and ends with arrival in the theater. USTRANSCOM, through AMC and MSC, operates the strategic modes of transport. USTRANSCOM assures ITV of forces, to include nonunit-related personnel and supplies. USTRANSCOM, using GTN, provides the required force tracking information necessary for decision making.

OTHER CONSIDERATIONS DURING DEPLOYMENT

3-73. Need lead in when this FM is updated.

CONUS HIGHWAY REGULATION

3-74. Highway regulation within CONUS is a function of the MOBCON. This is a HQDA/ FORSCOM/National Guard Bureau proponency. MOBCON assigns the responsibility for CONUS highway movements to a DMC in the SMCC of each state. As proposed, the DMC will become the convoy approval authority for all active and reserve component forces highway movements. Requests for convoy clearance flows from the unit to the UMC at each Army installation. Each installation forwards each request to the DMC in the state where the convoy begins. The DMC provides the moving unit with a convoy movement order which reserves road space for the unit. It also provides a detailed movement schedule and includes information on the route. The DMC receives all requests from reserve units.

3-75. Due to the DMC's close relationship to civil authorities in each state, the MOBCON initiative also proposes the DMC certify movements important or essential to National Defense. The DMC also issues clearance for units needing special permits for oversize or overweight loads. The DMC serves as the DOD representative to the state DOT for Emergency Highway Traffic Regulation and provides aid to units moving during mobilization and deployment.

OCONUS HIGHWAY REGULATION

3-76. Supporting CINCs establish highway regulation policies and procedures to move deploying forces from OCONUS POEs. As required, the CINC coordinates the policies and procedures with the proper HNS agencies.

COMMAND, CONTROL, COMMUNICATIONS, AND OTHER SYSTEMS

3-77. The purpose of the transportation management information system is to improve transportation processes, realize efficiency and economy, and promote ITV. The timeliness and accuracy of data within management systems depends on the communications systems used to convey the data throughout the system. It also depends on the frequency of data. Ideally, data entered into the system is saved throughout the automation continuum. Enhanced transportation management within the Army requires a seamless automated management system. This system includes assured communications, which support transportation functions from origin to destination. Existing and developing Joint and Army systems can help strategic level planners and mode operators in planning and executing strategic deployment. Appendix A contains detailed information for each of the systems.

SECTION III - Movement Control at the Operational Level of War

INTRODUCTION

3-78. Movement control at the operational level of war links the strategic and tactical levels of war movement control organizations. Its focus is on deployment, reception, and onward movement. It encompasses the synchronization of transportation assets deployed or available in an AO to sustain joint/combined campaigns and other military activities. Movement control organizations at this level direct their attention backward toward the strategic system as well as forward to the tactical system. Operational movement control may involve a CINC or a CJTF. The procedures described in the succeeding sections of this chapter apply regardless of the size or type of deployed force.

MOVEMENT CONTROL ORGANIZATIONS

3-79. Need lead in when this FM is updated.

THE JOINT TRANSPORTATION BOARD

3-80. The CINC may organize a JTB to review and deconflict policies, priorities, and apportionments of transportation assets. Though the JTB is not a day-to-day working organization, it meets as required to act on issues that surface to its level. It usually consists of representatives from the Service components, movement control agencies, and the Joint Force, J3, and J4. CINC's organize a JTB based on perceived transportation needs.

JOINT MOVEMENT CENTER

3-81. The CINC establishes a JMC to control force movement and sustainment. It has a peacetime nucleus organization, organized functionally. The JMC expands in proportion to the size of the force and the desires of the supported CINC. The JMC coordinates strategic movements with USTRANSCOM. It also oversees the execution of theater transportation priorities. The JMC conducts cyclic reviews of apportionment decisions and acts on emergency transportation requests. When there is no JTB, the JMC is the primary advisor to the CINC in the apportionment process. To aid in the planning process, the JMC identifies the variance between forecasted requirements and current capabilities. It expedites action and coordination for immediate movement requirements to assure effective and efficient use of transportation resources. The JMC is normally under the staff supervision of the joint senior logistics staff officer.

3-82. When the deploying force is a JTF, the commander may organize a JMC. JMCs for JTFs are not a peacetime-manned element. They are usually established in crisis from the movement control elements of the CJTF's peacetime Service HQ with augmentation from all Service components, the CINC, and USTRANSCOM. It is potentially formed using Army component movement control organizations. The JTF JMC manages intra-theater lift and performs strategic lift functions in coordination with the CINC's JMC.

The JMC Organization

3-83. A fully developed JMC might have a plans and programs division and an operations division, supported by an administrative section. As needed, advisory members from functional areas, which impact movement planning and execution, supplement the JMC.

Manning the JMC

3-84. The CINC may use Service component personnel resources to establish a JMC or request support from a supporting CINC. Manning requirements should provide liaison with HN authorities to coordinate use of available civil transportation assets and facilities. When expanding a JMC with Service component resources, the CINC considers the structure of the dominant force and unique movement control requirements. The CINC may also draw on reserve personnel to enlarge the JMC. Reserve augmentation personnel should have participated in exercises to assure they are familiar with the procedures of a joint force HQ.

OTHER TRANSPORTATION ORGANIZATIONS AT THE OPERATIONAL LEVEL OF WAR

3-85. Need lead in when this FM is updated.

US TRANSPORTATION COMMAND

3-86. USTRANSCOM normally sets up forward elements from each of the subordinate TCCs within the AO. These elements coordinate strategic transportation information with the supported CINC's JMC or staff. A USTRANSCOM movement control liaison cell also collocates with the operational level JMC to enhance the strategic movement control and coordination process.

AIR MOBILITY COMMAND

3-87. AMC is the USTRANSCOM component responsible for fulfilling strategic air mobility movement requirements that occur at the operational level of war. Execution of this mission is exercised through the TACC which is the AMC unit responsible for planning, tasking, and controlling operational air mobility mission meeting USTRANSCOM global responsibilities. During contingency operations, a DIRMOBFOR may be designated to manage the air mobility mission for a theater or, if established, a JTF. The DIRMOBFOR exercises execution management authority for theater assigned air mobility assets and will coordinate with the TACC in deconflicting and monitoring the movement of strategic air mobility assets within the theater.

MILITARY TRAFFIC MANAGEMENT COMMAND

3-88. MTMC operates common-user ocean terminals within CONUS. The command also operates common-user water terminals OCONUS, based on agreements negotiated with CINCs and the HNs. Normally, the CINC will use MTMC forward base terminal operations to support deployments. CINCs may also request MTMC support to operate water terminals in an area where MTMC has no presence. MTMC personnel may also be a part of the USTRANSCOM cell deployed to support the operational level movement control element.

MILITARY SEALIFT COMMAND

3-89. MSC usually establishes command and control elements at water terminals. They provide combatant commanders with strategic sealift and related management information.

ARMY OPERATIONAL LEVEL OF WAR MOVEMENT CONTROL

3-90. The Army fields an operational level movement control element that fits the size and the requirements of the deployed force. The size of the force may be a brigade, division, Corps, EAC, or a tailored task force. The DTO, in coordination with the DISCOM MCO, executes the movement control functions at division. The CTO, in coordination with the Corps MCC, accomplishes the movement control task at the Corps level. The ASCC transportation staff, in coordination with TAMCA, works for the ASCC when an EAC force deploys into the AO. If the Army deployed force is a tailored task force, the ASCC must provide resources to execute the functions of movement control.

3-91. Division and Corps movement control organizations may plan and execute functions at the operational level as well as the tactical level. However, their doctrinal organizations provide primarily for tactical operations. Consequently, the size and capabilities of movement control elements at brigade, division, and Corps may not be sufficient to manage the movement control functions at the operational level of war. In these instances, the ASCC should provide augmentation as required. Regardless of the size of the element executing movement control at this level of war, the functions remain the same.

3-92. The following covers the responsibility of the Army organization (TAMCA) which is designed to execute movement control operations at the operational level. A discussion of the tactical level of movement control operations at Corps and division appears in the movement control operations at the tactical level of this chapter.

THEATER ARMY MOVEMENT CONTROL AGENCY

3-93. The Army executes movement control for EAC at the operational level through a TAMCA. The TAMCA operates under the command and control of the ASCC. In some instances, this organization reports to the primary logistics staff officer in the ASCC staff. The TAMCA helps develop and executes the Army posture of the joint movement program developed by the JMC.

3-94. The TAMCA serves as the primary element for the planning and controlling of transportation operations at the operational level of war. The TAMCA synchronizes its operations with those of the JMC, USTRANSCOM, and lower echelon MCCs. It also follows the priorities established by the ASCC.

3-95. The TAMCA provides movement management services and highway traffic regulation to execute the reception and onward movement of forces, cargo, and personnel. It does so by positioning subordinate movement control battalions and their subordinate MCTs at critical nodes within the AO. The TAMCA, through its subordinate movement control organizations, has committal authority over the transportation assets assigned under the Army Support Command structure developed for the operation. It levies requirements on modes, but does not identify the specific asset that is to accomplish the mission. The TAMCA monitors the use of transportation assets throughout the AO and maintains a record of changes in terminal capabilities. The TAMCA helps negotiate the acquisition of additional transportation capability through contracts and HNS agreements. FM 55-10 contains additional information on Army movement control.

Movement Control Transportation Battalions

3-96. As required, movement control transportation battalions operate in assigned movement regions through the AO. The number of customers served, the number of modes and nodes programmed, and the geographical size of the AO determine the size of the regions. Transportation movement battalions are responsible to the TAMCA for the control and management of movements which takes place in their respective regions. MCTs, assigned to the battalions, help decentralize the execution of movement matters. They do this by being assigned on an area basis or at key transportation nodes. MCTs provide the users of transportation the point of entry into the transportation request system.

Movement Control Teams

3-97. MCTs are the common point of contact for mode operators and users of transportation. Their role is to accelerate, coordinate, and monitor traffic moving through the transportation system. MCTs are found at the operational and tactical levels of war based on the size of the supported force and the complexity of transportation operations. There are three types of MCTs. They provide flexibility in assignments based on forecasted workload. The three types of MCTs are as follows:

- *Movement control team.* The primary function of this team is to control the movement of personnel and materiel. They are also responsible for the coordination of bulk fuel and water transportation at pipeline and production take-off points.

- *Air terminal movement control team.* This team arranges transport, coordinates loading, and expedites the movement of personnel and materiel through Air Force and civilian air terminals.

- *Movement regulating team.* This team operates at critical terminals and at critical highway points. This team helps with the diversion of cargo and by troubleshooting movement control problems.

OPERATIONAL DEPLOYMENT PHASES

3-98. The focus of the operational level transportation system during the deployment phase is the reception and onward movement of units, personnel, and material. The focus of movement control is the same. To accommodate the intensity of the initial deployment, movement control units must be deployable and deploy early. Simultaneously, movement control and material management units must coordinate with the CINC's staff for force closure and for total battlefield distribution during the deployment phase to achieve integrated movement control and material management during the employment phase. Synchronized distribution planning is essential, as a poorly defined distribution pattern developed early will negatively effect total distribution later.

3-99. To assist movement control units during reception and onward movement, the Army provides additional temporary organizations for force reception. The two main organizations usually fielded are PSAs and A/DACGs. These organizations are provided by the deploying force and disband as the Army force transitions to routine personnel replacement and sustainment operations. Chapter 4 covers the operation of the PSAs and the A/DACGs. Refer to FM 55-65 for more detailed information.

PHASE 1 - THEATER RECEPTION

3-100. This phase begins when the forces and sustainment arrive at PODs in the AO. It occurs exclusively at the reception terminals. It involves the off-loading of vessels and aircraft, the linking of equipment with personnel, and the loading of equipment and personnel into modes for onward movement.

3-101. The reception of the force is the responsibility of the supported CINC. The ASCC operates the PODs assigned to the Army component. This includes the supervising of terminals manned by contracted personnel or coordinating those operated under HN agreements. USTRANSCOM, through agreements with the supported CINC, may operate terminals.

3-102. This phase ends when the forces leave the PODs. Appendix B contains a checklist of useful considerations for review by commanders when developing a reception plan.

PHASE 1 - THEATER ONWARD MOVEMENT

3-103. This phase begins when the force leaves the PODs. It occurs entirely in-transit and may involve en route stopovers. These stopovers provide the opportunity to arm, fuel, equip, and sustain the force. ITV and force tracking are crucial during this period.

3-104. The onward movement phase is the responsibility of the supported CINC. The CINC uses the JMC, supported by USTRANSCOM, to achieve ITV and force tracking. The ASCC, through its MCC, supports the effort.

3-105. During reception and onward movement phases, movement control units focus their activities on unit movement and ITV. However, the units must also coordinate transportation support for early arriving sustainment, life support functions, and other port clearance missions such as prepositioned afloat.

3-106. This phase ends when the force is delivered and ready to execute its mission to the commander who will direct their employment. This is normally at the TAA. Appendix B contains considerations for review by commanders when developing an onward movement plan.

THEATER MOVEMENT PROGRAM

3-107. The movement program is the plan used by the ASCC to plan and execute the reception and onward movement of units, personnel, equipment, and their sustainment. It is a living document that requires updating to accommodate known and anticipated transportation requirements. When done properly, the movement program defines the transportation system. It helps identify locations for terminals and provides for the best use of the available modes of transport. The operational level movement control element is responsible for developing the movement program.

3-108. There are eight steps used to develop the movement program. Transportation planners execute these steps concurrently and continuously. FM 55-10 contains a detailed discussion on the development of a movement program. The following information provides a summary of these steps. Figure 3-7, page 3-28, portrays their relationship.

Assessing the Distribution Pattern

3-109. The distribution pattern contains the complete logistic picture within the AO. The assessment is best done by determining the location of the nodes within the transportation system. The distribution pattern begins by locating PODs, transitioning through the staging areas, including the sites for supply and maintenance activities. It then concludes with the identification of sites for the terminals within the tactical AO. The completed distribution plan depicts how planners have assigned modes to link the terminals. The distribution pattern is used by transportation planners to identify destinations for transportation support and to indicate diversion sites. The distribution pattern constantly evolves as the theater matures and as the execution of the campaign plan progresses. It must consider intelligence and engineer information and must fit the commander's concept of the operation.

Determining Requirements

3-110. Transportation planners determine requirements by forecasting the quantities and types of supplies, mail, and personnel for movement in support of the operation. The users of the transportation system provide these requirements. The planners develop movement requirements by class of supply, estimated weight, and cube. They forecast priorities and plan origins and destinations. Users also identify special handling requirements, such as water, refrigerated, hazardous, or sensitive cargo. Personnel movements are grouped by categories such as troops, civilians, patients, and prisoners of war. The planners use cycles to determine requirements. For example, the initial planning may contain a projection of transportation requirements to assure establishing a lodgment. Once the situation stabilizes and the operation matures, experience shows that a 14-day planning period works best. This allows for a 7-day firm forecast and a 7-day tentative forecast for the succeeding period. However, planning periods should support the commander's concept of operations.

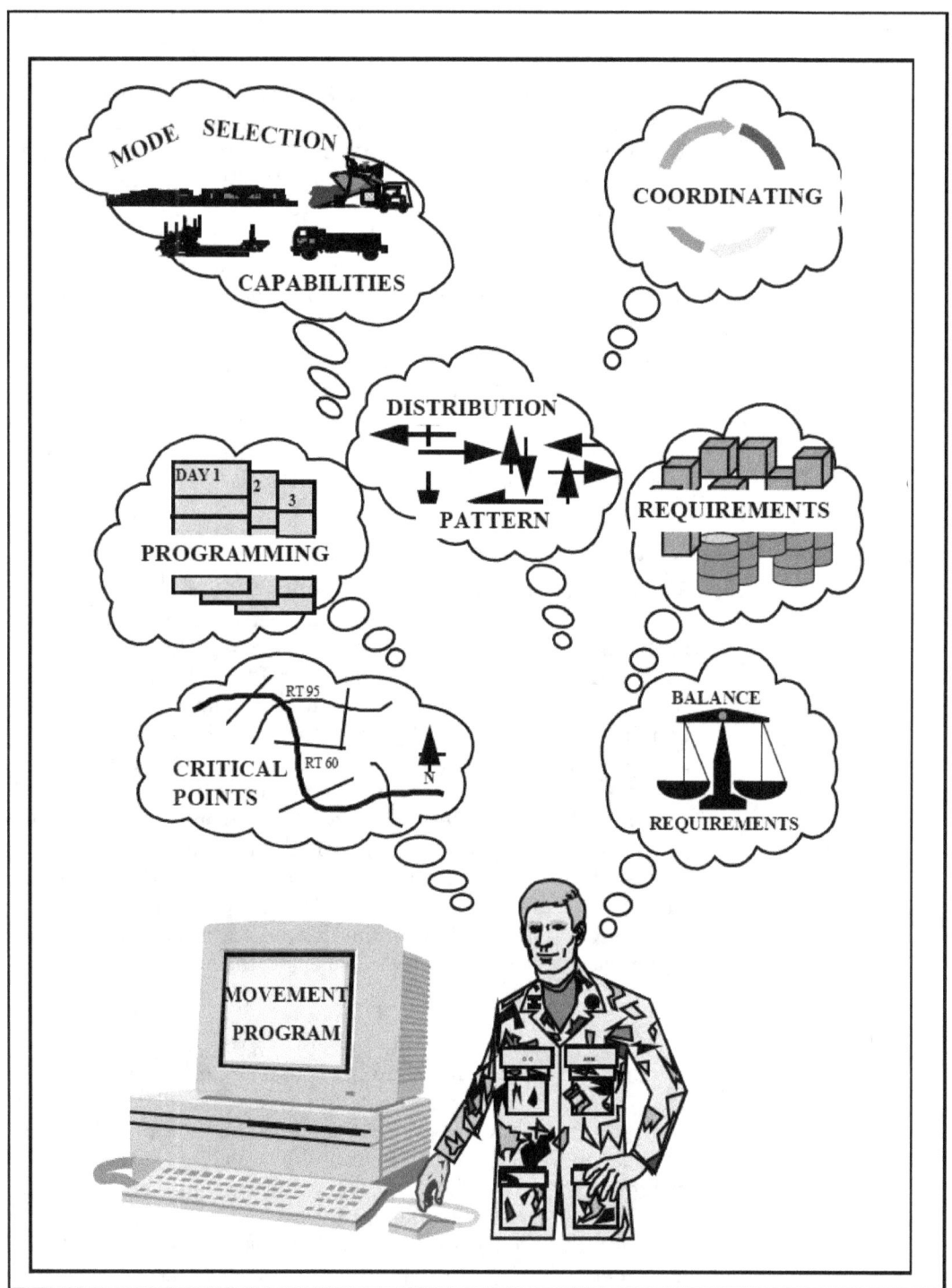

Figure 3-7. Movement Program Development

Determining Capabilities

3-111. This step involves the determination of the capabilities of the transportation system. It consists of two factors which include:

- The efficiency of the physical structures in the terminals.
- The availability of the operating units, contractor personnel, or HNS available to man the nodes and terminals.

When assessing these factors, planners should consider not only the capabilities available within the AO, but those the Army force has planned for deployment as well. The final tally should show the carrying capacity of the mode operators and the reception and clearance capability of the terminals. To accomplish this task, transportation planners also consider factors such as weather and terrain. FM 55-15 contains detailed planning factors to help determine the capabilities of modes and terminals.

Balancing Requirements Against Capabilities

3-112. By balancing the requirements against the capabilities, the transportation planner can determine if the modes and terminals available can support the commander's concept of the operation. The planner uses this data to distribute the Army workload among transportation mode and terminal operations and to seek changes in priorities or additional capability if a shortfall exists. When balancing requirements, the transportation planner must consider the command relationships, the geographical areas of responsibilities, and the risk of failure due to the tactical situation.

Determining Critical Points

3-113. Critical points within the transportation system exist at the nodes as well as in the links that connect the nodes. Planners base the evaluation of their criticality by determining if existing restrictions could slow down or stop movement. Restriction determination consists of analyzing the physical structures within the nodes and links. It also includes their subjectivity to enemy actions. Restriction factors also include the capability to man the nodes and the terminals. Transportation planners enlist the assistance of engineer and MP staff planners in the determination of critical points.

3-114. Transportation planners develop alternative plans and control measures to overcome congestion at critical points. The movement control element forecasts congestion and positions movement teams to respond to the delays. When required, MCTs coordinate with the tactical commander to assure the acquisition of security support.

Programming by Schematics

3-115. When time permits, transportation planners should use schematics to help balance requirements and capabilities. Schematics graphically portray the shipping requirements against capabilities. The two types of schematics planners can use are requirements and mode schematics. Each available mode uses mode schematics. When superimposed over maps, schematics provide a visual representation of the transportation system structure. FM 55-10 contains a detailed description on the preparation of schematics.

Selecting a Mode

3-116. When selecting or allocating modes, transportation planners consider the priority of the requirement. Planners must also rate other factors, such as the characteristics of the shipment, security, and political considerations. Planners should also consider eliminating the rehandling of cargo. If rehandling cannot be avoided, planners expedite the transition of cargo to the final destination. Chapter 5 of this manual contains a more detailed description of the considerations planners should follow when selecting a mode.

Coordinating

3-117. Coordinating the movement program is a continuous task. It involves movement of personnel and equipment, to include those involved in airlift, at all levels of war through extended LOC's across command AOR. It also involves coordinating with MP and engineer units responsible for supporting the transportation infrastructure. Coordination must achieve integrated planning and synchronized execution across levels of command. Coordinating also involves the users of the system. As shippers request transportation support from their local MCCs and MCTs, the program remains viable as changes become visible, early enough to assure transportation support.

OTHER CONSIDERATIONS

3-118. Planners also consider two other major aspects when developing the movement program. These are the development of a POD clearance program and establishing a highway regulation system.

The POD Clearance Program

3-119. The POD clearance program is a subset of the operational level movement program. However, PODs require close attention because they are nodes that can get congested easily. Transportation planners should develop a program specifically designed to handle the clearance program. FM 55-10 contains a detailed description on the preparation of a POD clearance program.

Highway Regulation

3-120. Highway regulation consists of planning, routing, scheduling, and deconflicting the use of road networks to facilitate movement. The extent of the regulation depends upon the number of moves and the capacity of the road networks. Highway regulation is crucial when operating over underdeveloped and saturated road networks. Freeflow of traffic allows for the maximum movement of cargo and personnel. However, transportation planners and operators should only use freeflow when the road network and security requirements allow.

3-121. Highway regulation is the responsibility of the commander having area jurisdiction. For example, the operational commander exercises this responsibility for the operational area and the tactical commander does the same in the tactical area. Commanders must assure that highway movements requirements are deconflicted and coordinated highway moves occur as listed in the movement program. Figure 3-8, page 3-32, illustrates the Highway Regulation Function. FM 101-5 and FM 55-10 contain information, which includes traffic circulation plans, useful in the development of highway regulation procedures.

RELATIONSHIP BETWEEN OPERATIONAL AND TACTICAL MOVEMENT CONTROL ORGANIZATIONS

3-122. The operational level movement control organization has responsibilities that go beyond geographic boundaries. It provides guidance and technical assistance to the movement control elements at the tactical level. The support consists of advice on the movement programs, policies, and procedures established by the ASCC. At times, operational level transportation assets are located in the tactical area. This requires a close working relationship between the respective movement control elements and subordinate MCTs. When required, the operational level movement control element may provide additional MCTs to support the tactical level movement control organization. An example is to establish first destination reporting points at the boundary between the operational and tactical level.

3-123. The operational level movement control organization receives forecasts of requirements from the tactical level organization. These forecasts include the priorities of the tactical commander. The operational level movement control organization also compiles and has available, the tactical level terminal cargo reception and processing capability.

SECTION IV - Movement Control at the Tactical Level of War

INTRODUCTION

3-124. Movement control at the tactical level of war is the responsibility of the tactical commander. The main Army tactical organizations are the Corps and the division. Each of these organizations has an organic movement control capability. This capability is augmented when operating at the operational level of war. When the smallest Army component in a joint force is a brigade, the ASCC provides resources to assure the execution of movement control functions.

3-125. Movement control at the tactical level also plays a key role in the development of the battlefield circulation and control plan. This plan deconflicts the maneuver force with the logistic units movement requirements. The plan is coordinated through the responsible MP and engineer organizations in the AO.

3-126. Movement control at the tactical level focuses on the final distribution of supplies and personnel. Final distribution arms, fuels, maintains, mans the units, and sustains the soldier.

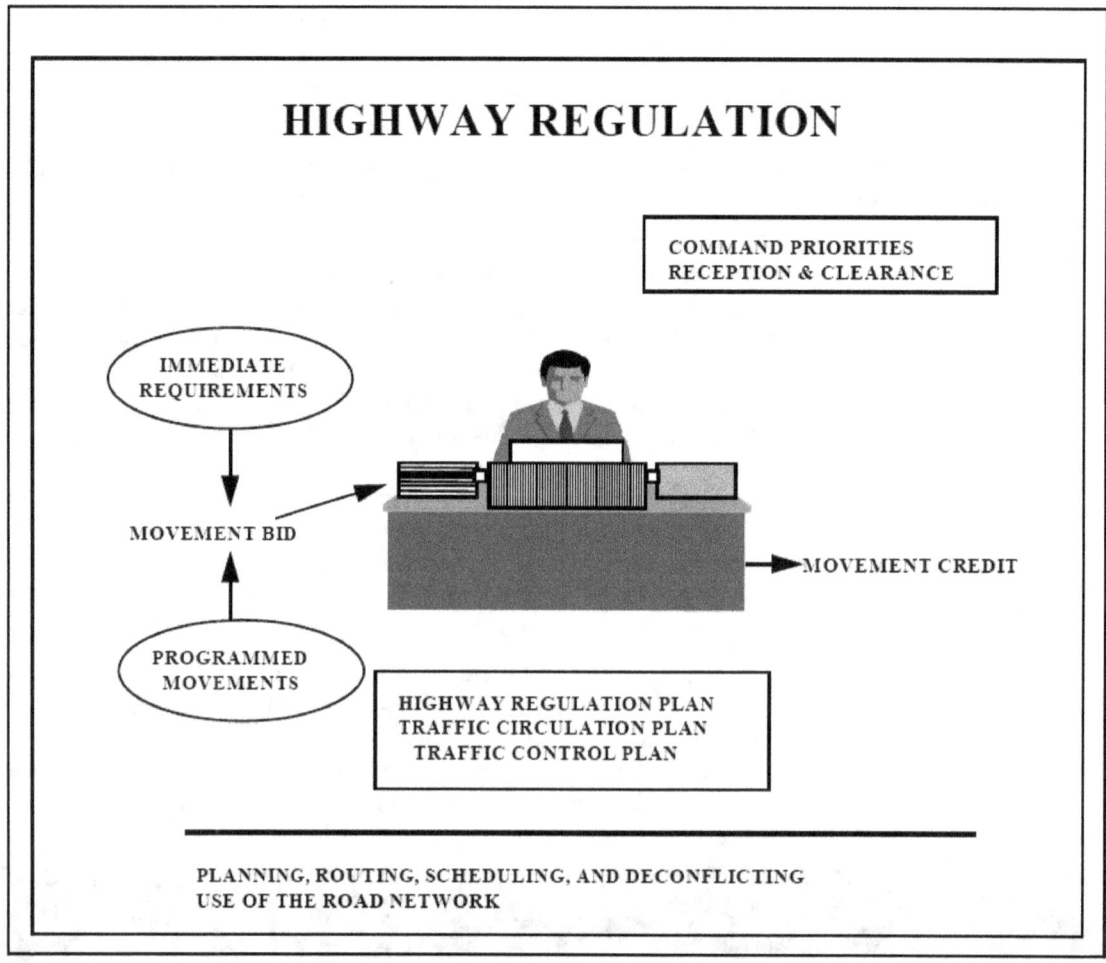

Figure 3-8. Highway Regulation Function

MOVEMENT CONTROL AT THE CORPS

3-127. The Corps G3 and G4 staffs and the COSCOM conduct movement planning. The G3 plans and directs maneuver and establishes priorities. The G4 exercises staff supervision for movements and oversees the fulfillment of the commander's logistics priorities. The G3 and G4 staffs receive support from the CTO in the execution of these tasks. The COSCOM develops and executes the Corps movement program. It does this by using, on a daily basis, the movement control, terminal, and mode resources organic to the Corps.

CORPS TRANSPORTATION OFFICER

3-128. The CTO is the Corps transportation staff planner. As a special staff officer, the CTO is assigned by the Chief of Staff to work for the Corps G3 or G4. The CTO assists the G3 during unit movement and maneuver planning. The CTO assists the G4 in the areas of logistic and unit movement requirements. As a staff officer responsible for transportation matters in the Corps, the CTO assesses the effectiveness of the movement program. He then recommends the types of transportation organizations required to accomplish the Corps mission. FM 55-10 contains a detailed discussion of the duties of the CTO.

CORPS MOVEMENT CONTROL CENTER

3-129. The Corps MCC provides centralized movement control and highway regulation in the Corps AO. It does this for personnel, mail, and materiel moving into, within, or out of the Corps area. The MCC also performs transportation planning and ITV for the Corps. The Corps MCC accomplishes its mission by using attached MCTs and MRTs.

3-130. The MCC commander normally positions teams, within rear and forward CSG, throughout the Corps area. The positioning is done to extend control of critical transportation nodes, facilities, or operating units. Allocation of teams normally includes one MCT per CSG and each critical transportation node in the Corps area. The MCC may also position ATMCTs at aerial ports located in the Corps AO. It may also place MRTs at key transportation nodes and other critical locations (congested areas) along MSRs.

3-131. The MCC has committal authority over transportation assets assigned to the CSGs. Committal authority is levying a requirement on a mode, not the identification of the asset. The MCC monitors transportation use within each CSG through its MCTs. If the MCC is the senior movement control element in the AO, it will help negotiate the acquisition of additional transportation capability through contracts and HNS agreements. The MCC develops a forecast of transportation requirements based on the priorities of the commander.

MOVEMENT CONTROL AT THE DIVISION

3-132. Movement control at the division includes planning for deployment and receiving and distributing cargo and personnel to the units. It is a staff responsibility since the division has no organic movement control organizations like those found in the Corps or at EAC. It also involves planning for the movement of units not committed to combat within the division area. Like at the operational level of war AOR , the division develops a system that identifies nodes within its AO. It also develops procedures to deliver personnel and supplies using the available modes. The division also develops a traffic circulation plan used to regulate the highways within its AOR. The movement control responsibility within the division is shared by the G3 and G4. The DTO executes the missions. FM 55-10 contains more information on division movement control operations.

DIVISION TRANSPORTATION OFFICER

3-133. At division level, the DTO functions as a special staff officer under the supervision of the Chief of Staff. The Chief of Staff has the option of placing the DTO under the supervision of the Division G3 or G4. The DTO has overall responsibility for movement control planning and highway regulation. The DTO plans for the movement of the division by all modes and executes movement control. He is also responsible for coordinating highway regulation plans with the division staff, the CTO, the Corps MCC, and the DISCOM MCO. The DTO normally delegates responsibility for mode management, movement programming, and transportation management within the division to the DISCOM MCO.

THE DIVISION SUPPORT COMMAND MOVEMENT CONTROL OFFICER

3-134. The MCO serves on the DISCOM commander's staff. He develops the division movement program and coordinates with the DMMC for the delivery of supplies and equipment. The MCO coordinates personnel and mail movement with the Division G1. The MCO coordinates and receives the priorities from the DTO. The MCO normally is located in the division rear with the DISCOM command post.

3-135. The MCO has commitment authority for truck assets assigned to the TMT company assigned to the DISCOM MSB. If the G3 has allocated aviation brigade assets for CSS, the MCO will have committal authority for those assets as well.

3-136. When the MCO or nondivisional units in the division rear need additional transportation assets, they submit a support request to the supporting MCT/MCC. If the CSG cannot provide the support, the MCT will pass the requirement to the Corps MCC. The Corps MCC will assess the transportation capability within other CSGs to support the requirement and commit the CSG that can best provide support.

SECTION V - Movement Control in Operations Other Than War

INTRODUCTION

3-137. FM 100-23 characterizes peace operations as an umbrella term encompassing observers, monitors, traditional peacekeeping, preventive deployment, security assistance, protection, and delivery of humanitarian relief. It also includes military support to civil authorities. Peace operations can guarantee rights of passage, impose sanctions, and enforce the peace. Although peace operations are clearly OOTW, many tasks at the tactical and operational levels of war may require the focused and sustained application of force.

3-138. The primary effort of many peace operations is logistics, and as such, transportation planning. Considerations include operating within the UN to support coalition forces and allies. Other considerations include working with personnel from nongovernmental agencies and private organizations and developing HN capability to provide support.

3-139. Movement control functions during peace operations are not materially different from those in other levels of conflict. Basic tasks and missions remain the same. However, these missions and tasks take place under the direction of the JFC, who establishes a CMOC to coordinate activities outside the military requirements of the operation. FM 100-23 and FM 100-23-1 contain more details on the conduct of operations for humanitarian assistance. The planning process at all command levels must involve transportation planners to determine the extent of the transportation and movement requirements. The transportation planners can then recommend the force structure required to support the requirements during deployment, employment, and redeployment.

3-140. Movement control requirements will vary based on the mission and number and types of units deployed. FM 55-10 has more information about movement control in other operational environments.

Chapter 4

Army Terminal Operations

Need lead in when this FM is updated.

INTRODUCTION

4-1. Army terminal operations involve receiving, processing, and staging passengers. It also includes receiving, loading, transferring, and discharging unit equipment and cargo. The main activities executed at terminals are loading and unloading modes of transport, marshaling, manifesting, stow planning loads, and documenting movement through the terminal. Some terminals can provide transit storage.

4-2. Terminals are key nodes in the total distribution system that supports the commander's concept of operation at all levels of war and through the range of military operations. When linked by modes of transport, they define the transportation structure for the operation. Force projection missions require the early identification and establishment of terminals. A well conceived plan assures that terminals can support the deployment, reception, and onward movement of the force and its sustainment. Crucial to the execution of the operation is the assignment of the right cargo and MHE at each terminal. ITV of materiel flowing through the terminals also provides the supported CINC with information pertaining to location and final destination of all cargo.

4-3. The two broad categories of terminals are water and inland terminals. Water terminals are established at ports, beach sites, or degraded/unimproved facilities. Inland terminals include facilities such as air terminals, truck terminals, TTPs, rail yards, and inland water terminals. Commanders establish inland terminals at points along air, rail, rivers and canals, pipelines, and motor transport LOC to provide for the transshipment of cargo and personnel carried by these modes.

4-4. Terminals are also classified based on the physical facility, the general type of cargo they handle, and the methods used for cargo handling. Classifying terminals aids in determining their cargo capacity. Knowing the cargo capacity of terminals helps to develop a plan to support the military operation.

PHYSICAL FACILITY

4-5. Terminals, classified by their physical facility, fall in two categories (fixed and unimproved). Examples of fixed terminals are deep-draft vessel capable piers, established paved transient facilities with warehouse space, and an existing airfield. Examples of unimproved terminals are bare beaches and inland terminals set up to operate from unpaved surfaces and without overhead cover. Transportation planners should seek to use fixed facilities for terminals. If time and the situation allows, the CINC should also negotiate improvements of the terminal infrastructure in potential areas of operation before the deployment of the force.

CARGO HANDLING METHOD

4-6. Terminals are also classified by method of cargo handling. This classification includes containers, RO/RO, breakbulk, LO/LO, and lighterage. By using the cargo handling criteria, planners can determine the units and MHE needed to operate a terminal.

TYPES OF CARGO

4-7. The type of cargo handled is another way to classify terminals. The types of cargo include ammunition, explosives, bulk fuel, and other hazardous cargo. Establishing hazardous cargo terminals usually requires the calculation of quantity safety-distance factors. The requirement to store classified materiel and personal and official mail is another important consideration.

SECTION I - Types of Terminals

WATER TERMINALS

4-8. The availability and capabilities of water terminals is essential to the success of a military operation. Water terminals used as departing ports are called SPOE. Water terminals used as arriving ports are called SPOD. Commanders consider distances, the OPSEC plan, and the terminal capabilities when selecting a departure water terminal. The selection of arrival water terminals is equally important to the success of a military operation. Destination water terminals are crucial to establishing a lodgment and to sustaining the deployed force.

4-9. Water terminal operations are conducted at fixed, unimproved, or bare beach port facilities. One of the main objectives is to maximize the throughput of cargo. Maximizing throughput may require the military force to use a combination of terminals over time, while improving existing facilities. FM 55-60 contains more information on the establishment and operation of Army terminals.

FIXED WATER TERMINALS

4-10. Fixed water terminals permit deep-draft vessels to berth and discharge cargo directly onto a pier or quay. The cargo may move to in-transit storage areas to await terminal clearance. Another option is loading the cargo directly onto surface transport, to include rail, for onward movement. Fixed water terminals normally have a high degree of sophistication in facilities, equipment, and organization to support cargo handling, container operations, and port clearance operations.

UNIMPROVED WATER TERMINALS

4-11. An unimproved water terminal is a site with significant shortcomings that hinder operations. These may include fixed water terminals that have significant damage that may also hinder operations. An unimproved water terminal does not have the facilities, equipment, or infrastructure of a fixed water terminal. The characteristics of an unimproved water terminal facility are insufficient water depth, lack of installed MHE, and not enough berthing space to accommodate deep-draft cargo vessels. Vessel discharge normally occurs at anchor using lighterage. The Army uses unimproved facilities when fixed water terminals are not available or to increase throughput to meet requirements.

BARE BEACH TERMINALS

4-12. Bare beach terminals use lighterage and/or causeways to move cargo across a beach or to the shore. These operations are known as LOTS. LOTS may include the establishment of an off-shore petroleum discharge system. However, a LOTS operation does not refer to bare beach operations only. LOTS also applies to stream discharge operations conducted from ship anchorage sites. An example of this type of operation is ocean-going ships discharging cargo to lighterage for movement to a bare beach or to an improved terminal or unimproved terminal.

4-13. Beach facilities require selected sites to enable lighterage to move cargo to or across the beach into marshaling yards. Bare beach operations occur under less than desirable conditions. They require significant engineer support to prepare access routes to and from the beach. Landing craft, amphibians, and terminal units conduct beach operations. When the Army operates a bare beach terminal, the operation remains under the command and control of a transportation terminal battalion. The supported CINC determines what Service component has command and control of JLOTS. The Army uses bare beach facility operations when no other terminal facilities are available or to augment throughput capability at fixed terminals.

CONTAINER TERMINALS

4-14. Container terminals are facilities designed for uninterrupted, high-volume flow of containers between ship and inland transportation modes. Fixed port facilities normally have the capability to handle containers. Container terminals serve specialized, largely nonself-sustaining vessels. Gantry cranes, shoreside support structures, and associated MHE are available at water terminals designed to move containers.

ROLL-ON/ROLL-OFF TERMINALS

4-15. RO/RO terminals have special purpose ramps designed to handle vehicles that can load or discharge under their own power. Because of the rapid accumulation of equipment at pier-side, RO/RO terminals should have an open hard surface with sufficient space to support the marshaling of convoys. RO/RO is the best method to use when handling unit rolling stock. Fixed port facilities normally have a RO/RO capability.

BREAKBULK TERMINALS

4-16. Breakbulk terminal operations involve palletized or specially packaged cargo, unitized for ease of handling, but not in containers. As a minimum, the berth of breakbulk terminals should have an apron for the full length of the ship and be wide enough to support MHE operations. Breakbulk is the least desirable method of handling military cargo through a terminal because it is time consuming, MHE dependent, and manpower intensive. Fixed port facilities usually have breakbulk capability.

4-17. This type terminal supports LO/LO operations. Extensive planning is required, specifically if the LO/LO operation involves the handling of flatracks and cargo loaded in sea-sheds.

LIGHTERAGE TERMINALS

4-18. Lighterage terminal operations use self-propelled and/or towed floating craft to carry cargo between vessels at anchor and the shore or pier off-load site. Lighterage operations are inherently hazardous, complex, and time consuming. Lighterage terminals are normally associated with unimproved or bare beach facilities.

4-19. The Army uses lighterage terminal operations only when no other capability is available, when moving cargo through inland waterways to inland terminals, or to augment other ongoing cargo-handling operations. The Army also uses lighterage at fixed port facilities when no berthing space for a ship is available. Some equipment used to perform these operations include SEABEE, LASH barges, commercial self-propelled and towed barges, and landing craft. Lighterage terminals operations can handle containerized, breakbulk, or RO/ RO cargo.

INLAND WATER TERMINALS

4-20. The Army establishes inland water terminals along waterways. These terminals serve a dual purpose. They receive, load, and unload cargo destined to locations accessible to and from the water terminal. They also provide for the maintenance of the watercraft and rest for the crew.

INLAND TERMINALS

4-21. Inland terminals may be used to complement an existing transportation network to move cargo. They can greatly reduce congestion and the workload of the modes. Traditional examples of inland terminals include air terminals, motor transport terminals, and rail terminals. Other commonly known facilities such as Army installations, depots, central receiving points, and supply support activities are also considered inland terminals. Inland terminals also provide facilities for connecting links of the same modes when the situation dictates a change in carrier. In emergency situations, in-transit storage is provided at origin, intermediate, destination terminals, or TTPs.

AIR TERMINALS

4-22. An air terminal is a facility that functions as an air transportation hub and accommodates the loading and unloading of aircraft and in-transit processing of traffic. Air terminals can support several types of operations. These operations are support to unit movements, common-user sustainment, and personnel replacement. Selecting departure and arrival air terminals are crucial to the success of a force projection military operation. FM 100-27 contains more information on air terminals.

TRUCK TERMINAL/TRAILER TRANSFER POINT

4-23. The Army establishes truck terminals and TTPs along MSRs (to include POL sites) to accomplish line-haul or motor transport relay operations. Truck terminals are normally located where truck companies and their motor pools are positioned in the AO. These locations are near centers of concentrated trucking activities at both ends and along the way of the line-haul operation. TTPs are established at intermediate locations between truck terminals. These terminals include provisions for the assembly and dispatch of motor transport equipment. They also may provide a maintenance capability to service equipment including refrigerated containers. FM 55-30 contains more information on establishing truck terminals and TTPs.

RAIL TERMINALS

4-24. Rail terminals are facilities normally found at the beginning, along, or at the end of a rail line. Rail yards are also terminals, although usually not capable of loading and unloading cargo or personnel. Rail yards provide a capability to assemble trains, switch cars, and perform some minor maintenance.

4-25. Rail terminals usually have service facilities, freight, and passenger stations. At Service facilities, rail personnel can inspect and repair tracks and service engines with fuel and water. They can also use scales to weigh railcars before their movement to another destination. At freight and passenger stations, the terminal handles cargo and personnel. FM 55-20 contains more information on the operation of a rail terminal.

SECTION II - Terminal Operations Planning

INTRODUCTION

4-26. Staff planning and coordinating determines the numbers, types, and locations of terminals at all levels of war. This effort is vital to the development of the distribution system. USTRANSCOM selects terminals at the strategic level of war. USTRANSCOM coordinates the selection of CONUS terminals at the strategic level of war with the CINCs. The supported and supporting CINC transportation staff, working closely with the Service components and USTRANSCOM, plans and coordinates the selection of terminals at the operational level of war. The tactical commander selects terminals at the tactical level of war.

4-27. Planning for the optimization of terminals in the transportation system involves the following five-step process:

- Computing the terminal workload required to support the operation, expressing it as cargo tonnage per day.

- Estimating the available terminal capacity, which is the total tonnage that can be received, processed, and cleared through the terminal per day.

- Estimating construction requirements, which are the requirements for repair, rehabilitation, or new construction of facilities necessary to increase the terminal capacity to equal the required terminal workload.

- Estimating equipment requirements, which is the amount of equipment needed to process the required workload through the terminal with maximum efficiency.

- Estimating personnel requirements, which are the units and individuals needed for the operation of the terminal.

PLANNING FOR THE ESTABLISHMENT OF WATER TERMINALS

4-28. History shows that about 95 percent of unit equipment and sustainment cargo moves by sealift. The use of sealift requires the availability of water terminals. Therefore, planners must understand that water terminals are key to meeting the objectives of a force projection operation. If needed for the insertion of reinforcements and sustainment, water terminals should be among the key initial objectives seized during a forcible entry. Planners should work to locate water and air terminals in close proximity. Without adequate water terminals, the insertion and sustainment of the force and the capability to support a lodgement may become extremely difficult. The Army may operate water terminals in either a single Service or common-user environment. The Army must also have the capability to take over the entire water terminal operation in countries with no effective capability.

4-29. The purpose of water terminal operations is to place equipment and supplies where and when needed. The planners consider and determine the desired flow from origin to destination and return. This flow requires coordination between the strategic and operational level of war transportation organizations.

4-30. The efficient flow of equipment and supplies through water terminals is a key element of sustainment. To assure success, the terminal units scheduled to open a terminal arrive early and off-load first. The MHE required to handle prepositioned afloat vessels must be accessible and ready to come off the ship before any other off-loading operation.

4-31. Planners should establish terminals capable of handling palletized, containerized, bulk liquid, and RO/RO cargo. The capability to handle palletized, containerized, and RO/ RO reduces transit time. Planners should also consider creating a redundancy of terminals in the AO. This redundancy can provide different ways to process cargo and increase the cargo tonnage handled in support of the operation.

PLANNING FOR THE ESTABLISHMENT OF INLAND TERMINALS

4-32. Inland terminals provide flexibility and increase the capability of the transportation system to handle cargo. Planners establish them at sites that can support inland water-ways, motor, rail, and air transport modes. When established, the terminals and the nodes that link them should form LOC that flows from origin to destination. When possible, transportation planners should use and incorporate existing terminal facilities into the transportation distribution network. Terminals serving rail and inland waterways are examples of existing facilities. Figure 4-1 shows a generic schematic layout of terminals within an AO.

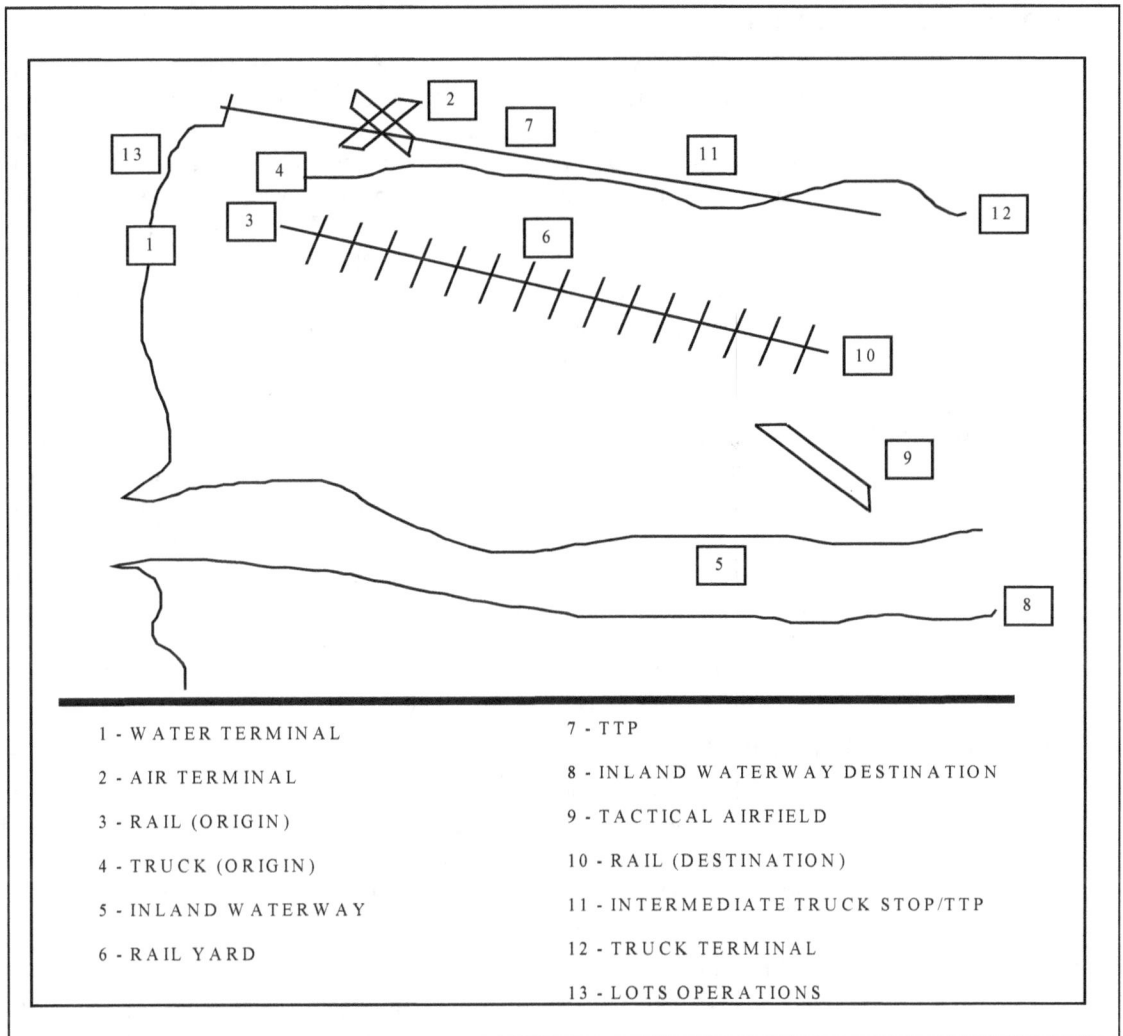

Figure 4-1. Generic Schematic Layout of Terminals Within an AO

1 - WATER TERMINAL	7 - TTP
2 - AIR TERMINAL	8 - INLAND WATERWAY DESTINATION
3 - RAIL (ORIGIN)	9 - TACTICAL AIRFIELD
4 - TRUCK (ORIGIN)	10 - RAIL (DESTINATION)
5 - INLAND WATERWAY	11 - INTERMEDIATE TRUCK STOP/TTP
6 - RAIL YARD	12 - TRUCK TERMINAL
	13 - LOTS OPERATIONS

ESTIMATION OF THROUGHPUT CAPACITY

4-33. Estimating terminal throughput capacity is key to the process of selecting terminal sites and operating units. The throughput capacity of a terminal is the lowest value of the reception, discharge, transfer, storage, and clearance capacity as described below. The throughput capacity of a terminal is dependent on its storage and clearance capacity. FM 55-60 contains a computation example.

TERMINAL RECEPTION CAPACITY

4-34. The type and sufficiency of operating space available to perform terminal operations determines the reception capacity of the terminal. This means sufficient space to stage cargo and modes of transport and while awaiting the processing of cargo and personnel. For example, important reception factors for water terminals include the number, size and type of piers or wharfs available, water depth, anchorage capacities, beach gradients, and the capability to satisfy special requirements for vessels containing hazardous cargo. The type and sufficiency of parking, warehousing, work space available for aircraft, rail cars, and motor transport assets usually dictate the reception capacity for inland terminals.

TERMINAL DISCHARGE CAPACITY

4-35. Terminal discharge capacity is the amount of personnel and materiel that can be received and off-loaded over a specified time. Discharge capacity is expressed in TEU (for containers), tons, barrels, square feet, or in numbers of personnel over a proper unit of time. Discharge or off-load capacity is normally a function of the available work force size. Discharge capacity is also affected by the physical facilities and specialized cargo handling equipment available at the terminal.

TERMINAL TRANSFER CAPACITY

4-36. Terminal transfer capacity consists of the activities required to transship personnel and cargo. Transshipment occurs at all types of terminals. Transshipment usually includes segregating, coopering, holding, documenting, and staging or storing, whenever a change in mode operator or carrier occurs.

TERMINAL STORAGE CAPACITY

4-37. Cargo storage capacity is the amount of cargo that can be stored at any one time. Storage capacity is expressed in square feet, MBBL, MTONs, number of TEU, or net explosive weight. When storage space is not available, major interruptions of terminal operations occur. Ideally, cargo unloading, processing, and reloading between various transportation modes takes place without interruption.

TERMINAL CLEARANCE CAPACITY

4-38. Terminal clearance capacity measures the ability to move cargo from the terminal to its first destination. It is measured in terms of tonnage, TEU, equipment driveaway, bulk liquid clearance measures, or numbers of personnel per unit of time. The first destination may be the final destination or another terminal.

TERMINAL THROUGHPUT CAPACITY

4-39. All capacities described above help the planner determine terminal throughput capacity. All capacities are considered, even if the limiting capacity is obvious. These estimates make it possible to determine the improvements that can generate the greatest increase in throughput capacity. Other considerations such as the threat, weather, and the availability of labor also must be taken into account. One of these factors may become the dominating factor. Table 4-1, pages 4-9 and 4-10, shows a sample checklist for estimating water terminal throughput capacity.

Table 4-1. Water Terminal Throughput Estimation Checklist

Collect these data:	Compute these factors:	To determine:
Channel depth Channel width Length of berths Type of berths (such as quay, pier, and mole) Diameter of anchorages Depth of water at berth Type of terminal at berth	Evaluate to determine water terminal reception capacity	
Discharge equipment on board Discharge equipment ashore Width of apron Special lift equipment Number of discharge equipment	Evaluate to determine water terminal discharge capacity	Water terminal throughput capacity for importing cargo only. (Retrograde operations will reduce the import capacity.)
Type of cargo Type of cargo-handling equipment Round-trip distance Number of cargo-handling equipment	Evaluate to determine water terminal transfer capacity	

Table 4-1. Water Terminal Throughput Estimation Checklist (continued)

Collect these data:	Compute these factors:	To determine:
Intrinsic capacity Average dwell time Operating capacity Terminal facilities Stacking methods Equipment used	Evaluate to determine water terminal storage capacity	
Clearance conveyance by mode Terminal equipment and personnel Gate capacity	Evaluate to determine water terminal clearance capacity	

NOTE: Once all of the above evaluations are completed, then the following should be applied: threat assessment, effect of the elements, and training level of labor.

SECTION III - Terminal Operations at the Strategic Level of War

INTRODUCTION

4-40. USCINCTRANS operates the strategic water and air terminals used as POEs and PODs within CONUS. USCINCTRANS selects the strategic terminals in coordination with the supported and supporting combatant commanders, the Service components, and the JCS. CINCs operate terminals in their AOR and select those to support a strategic deployment in support of a supported CINC. CINCs coordinate the selection of terminals with USCINCTRANS. USCINCTRANS may operate a terminal in an OCONUS AO after executing agreements with the proper CINC.

USTRANSCOM (MTMC) OPERATED WATER TERMINALS

4-41. USCINCTRANS selects CONUS water terminals and delegates their operation to MTMC. MTMC uses its organic organizations and reserve units to operate the terminals. MTMC operates several common-user military water terminals and outports for routine peacetime cargo shipments.

4-42. To accommodate the surge of cargo during unit deployments, MTMC opens several "expansion ports." These ports normally come under the command and control of TTBs. MTMC is the coordinating link between deploying units and their specific POEs. It prepares and issues port call messages for personnel and equipment and provides all SPOE stevedoring functions. Deploying units usually move to SPOEs by highway and rail. The deploying unit is responsible for arranging en route stops to provide for crew rest and refueling. MTMC arranges for commercial highway and rail movements, to include the use of terminals, en route to the SPOE. The deploying unit usually provides security for rail moves to SPOEs.

4-43. When required, MTMC also sends a DSB to the installation and requires the ASCC to organize and provide a PSA. DSB and PSA operations are discussed later in this chapter.

As a result of experiences during Operation Desert Shield/Storm and the shorter deployment objectives established within by the Army Strategic Mobility Program, MTMC created the WDIP. The objective of WDIP is to improve the terminal interface among the deploying units, supporting installations, FORSCOM, and MTMC. WDIP uses improved communications, realistic unit movement training, refined deployment procedures, and smoother execution of future deployments to accomplish its objectives. The basic element of the WDIP is a series of installation visits by MTMC and FORSCOM personnel to address key issues such as deployment planning, installation outloading, port operations, PSAs, sealift availability, scheduling, transportation automation and documentation, and certification of hazardous material.

TRANSPORTATION TERMINAL BATTALION OR BRIGADE

4-44. The TTB is a reserve unit that mobilizes upon receipt of the execute order. TTBs normally operate at established commercial port facilities, using contracted stevedores. The TTB provides traffic management and monitors commercial contracts for the movement of DOD cargo, including unit equipment, resupply, and retrograde shipments. Although TTBs are assigned to a specific port, they can operate at any designated SPOE. TTBs provide MTMC with the capability to expand the number of ports and to sustain SPOE operations. At the request of a supported or supporting CINC, FORSCOM and MTMC can deploy TTBs to operate an OCONUS water terminal.

DEPLOYMENT SUPPORT BRIGADES

4-45. DSBs are TDA RC units. They are made up of several individual UMTs. The teams can help deploying units at their location. When mobilized, DSBs fall under the command authority of MTMC. MTMC directs the DSB's UMTs to the designated installations. UMTs then establish liaison with the deploying unit transportation representative, movement control organization, and/or the ITO.

4-46. The DSB provides liaison and coordination for movement of port-called units to designated terminals. The liaison includes movement schedules; documentation; special cargo-handling requirements; hazardous, sensitive, and nonstandard configuration equipment; and any other information needed for deployment through the SPOE. UMTs do not actually document or load equipment.

PORT SUPPORT ACTIVITY

4-47. The PSA is a provisional organization formed by the deploying unit or its support force as directed by the ASCC. Its purpose is to support the terminal commanders in the loading and discharge of the equipment. Since the requirements vary between shipments, the ASCC tailors each PSA to fit the situation. Among the activities a PSA performs are driving special equipment and providing a trouble-shooting maintenance capability. PSAs operate almost exclusively in the terminal staging area. A MOU between the ASCC and MTMC identifies support requirements. The PSA is under the operational control of the terminal commander.

PORT SECURITY COMPANIES

4-48. PSCs provide close-in internal security for classified operating areas and sensitive logistical facilities including operation of specialized physical security devices. The PSC is a RC unit, that when mobilized, is under the command authority of MTMC. The USCG also has reserve port authority security attachments that when activated, operate under the operational command of the Naval Component Commander.

SUPERCARGOS

4-49. Supercargos refer to unit personnel that accompany, supervise, guard, and maintain their unit equipment on board a ship. Supercargos provide maintenance support and liaison during cargo reception at the SPOE and during shipload and discharge operations. They also support port clearance operations. The ASCC of the deploying force nominates and organizes Army supercargos for deployment.

4-50. While the exact composition of the supercargo team is dependent on several factors, the team ideally includes qualified mechanics. Supercargos are also licensed and experienced on each type of vehicle they are accompanying. When more than one organization deploys on a ship, the ASCC specifies who will provide the OIC and NCOIC.

OCONUS SUPPORTING CINC WATER TERMINALS

4-51. OCONUS CINCs are designated supporting CINCs to support an operation not located in their geographical AOR. Under these circumstances, supporting CINCs establish similar procedures as those described for CONUS. These procedures include the provision of PSAs, port security, and supercargos. When MTMC operates the terminals, the supporting CINC coordinates the procedures with USTRANSCOM and MTMC.

OTHER SERVICE COMPONENT WATER TERMINALS

4-52. Other Services operate strategic water terminals. ASCC of the deploying force coordinates with terminal commanders from other Services following the same procedures as those followed for Army operated terminals. Although these terminals operate in much the same manner as USTRANSCOM/MTMC terminals, there may be minor differences in procedures.

CONUS INLAND TERMINALS

4-53. At the strategic transportation level, inland terminals include activities such as Army installations, depots, and air terminals. These terminals are evaluated and selected during the planning process. Deploying units use these terminals during practice deployments.

US ARMY INSTALLATIONS AND DEPOTS

4-54. Installations and depots are the dominant terminals of origin for strategic deployments. Personnel, equipment, and supplies first experience the DTS at these locations. Depots usually have well developed rail and truck terminals to handle bulk shipments for sustainment and resupply. Unlike depots, installations are seldom staffed to accomplish the physical terminal activities. Deploying units provide the bulk of the manpower required for the preparation and out-loading of unit equipment. The installations provide the deploying units with blocking, bracing, and packing materials required to prepare their shipments. AR 55-355 stipulates the shipping and receiving capabilities for CONUS Army installations and depots. Regional CINCs prepare transportation facility guides for their AO.

USTRANSCOM (AMC) OPERATED AIR TERMINALS

4-55. AMC is the USTRANSCOM Air Force component command and is responsible for operating, or arranging for the operation of, all CONUS air terminals. AMC and contracted aircraft use these terminals to support Army organizations.

4-56. The Air Force usually positions a TALCE at the designated air terminal to oversee operations. The Air Force is responsible for providing the specialized MHE to load and off-load cargo and personnel from the aircraft. The deploying Army units provide pusher vehicles, shoring, and other MHE required to bring the cargo to its loading site or to clear the terminal.

4-57. Typically, units will deploy most of their personnel by air from their supporting airfield or from the nearest designated aerial port. The unit's equipment normally deploys by sea. Unit personnel will link-up with their equipment at their destination SPOD. Although the majority of unit equipment normally moves by sealift, some high priority equipment moves by air.

4-58. The ASCC coordinates the movement of Army personnel and cargo into and out of designated air terminals. The ASCC bases the coordination on information received from USTRANSCOM. The responsible movement control organization usually notifies the units about impending moves. Army units can expect that AMC will consolidate cargo at predesignated CONUS aerial terminals to maximize the productivity of the airlift system.

ARMY OPERATIONS AT AMC AIR TERMINALS

4-59. Army transportation support at air terminals assist with the deployment, redeployment, and sustainment of Army forces. Normally, an Army A/DACG assists the TALCE or MST in processing, loading, and off-loading deploying and arriving Army personnel and equipment. ATMCTs are designed to sustain A/DACG type operations for longer periods of time. By order of the ASCC, ATMCTs may replace A/DACG, as required.

Arrival/Departure Airfield Control Groups

4-60. A/DACGs are provisional organizations created to operate for a specific time or mission. They are not TOE units. The ASCC may direct personnel from deploying units, supporting organizations, installation staff, or other commands to form the A/DACGs. If required, the ASCC disbands the A/DACG or replaces it with a terminal transfer capability or an ATMCT for movement control purposes, when the specific period of operation has passed or the mission is completed. The duties of an A/DACG are described in FM 55-12.

Air Terminal Movement Control Teams

4-61. ATMCTs are transportation movement control TOE organizations assigned to transportation battalions (MC) or Corps MCCs. They operate primarily at Air Force terminals to support all Army sustainment requirements. ATMCTs perform movement control functions at air terminals. They will normally be assigned to an air terminal when:

- An airfield is designated an aerial port for the sustained air movement of personnel and material and to serve as an authorized APOE/APOD in a theater of operation.

- An airfield serves both unit movement and nonunit movement personnel and sustainment flow.

- The theater is joint or combined with multiple users of limited common-user transportation assets. FM 55-10 contains more information on the operations of the ATMCT.

SECTION IV - Terminal Operations at the Operational Level of War

INTRODUCTION

4-62. Operational level of war terminals are those operated in the AO. Certain operational level terminals are the entry point into or departure point from the AO and the initial points for theater distribution. They are typically located at ISBs, SPODs, APODs, supply support activities, and in-transit transfer points. Terminals must link to modes of transport to ensure the continuous flow of personnel and cargo.

4-63. The supported CINC and Service component commands select entry or departure point terminals at the operational level of war. The CINC usually retains the authority to select the POEs and PODs. The CINC coordinates the selection with USTRANSCOM and subordinate Service components.

4-64. The supported CINC normally delegates the responsibility for the selection and operation of inland terminals to the proper Service component commanders. As an example, the CINC will normally assign operational air terminal responsibilities to the AFSCC and operational water terminal operations to the Army or Navy Component Commander. The CINC may also opt to enter into an agreement with USCINCTRANS to allow MTMC to operate selected POE/POD water terminals. The selection and operation of terminals may require coordination with HN and allied transportation authorities.

4-65. The ASCC recommends to the CINC the types and quantities of units necessary to operate the designated Army terminals.

ARMY TERMINAL ORGANIZATIONS

4-66. Transportation planners choose from among a variety of Army transportation units to operate the terminals in the area of operation. These organizations are designed to provide maximum flexibility. They allow a planner to fit the units to the commander's concept of the operation by matching them with the size of the force deployed and the characteristics of the terminals available.

4-67. To provide command and control for the terminal units, the transportation structure provides a Army TRANSCOM, a transportation composite group, and an active duty TTB. A TRANSCOM provides command and control of two or more composite groups. The transportation composite group, the most likely element to deploy for command and control purposes, can manage two or more terminal battalions. The Army strategic mobility plan contingency corps requires support from a transportation composite group. The composite group may also support an independent division. When the size of the force is less than a division, an active duty TTB may be the senior Army terminal activity in the AO.

4-68. The organizations discussed above usually command and control the modes of transport available in the AO as well as the terminal units. Appendix C contains a description of the units a transportation planner should consider when selecting terminal units to fit a military operation.

WATER TERMINAL OPERATIONS, PLANNING AND EXECUTION CONSIDERATIONS

4-69. The planning and execution of water terminal operations at the operational level of war requires a detailed analysis of a wide range of factors. The factors include the following:

- Overall concept of the operation.
- Logistics support requirements.
- Physical characteristics and layout of the port and/or beaches.
- Relative location of highway, rail, air, and inland waterway networks.
- Location of supported and supporting units.
- Required repair and rehabilitation of existing facilities.
- Requirement for new construction.
- Requirement for security, especially if HNS is not available.

4-70. In a theater of operations, water terminals are located at one or more fixed port facilities, unimproved port facilities, or bare beaches. JLOTS operations also may be present in the theater.

4-71. Operational level of war water terminals introduce unit equipment (to include bulk fuel) into the AO and continue operations to sustain the force. During initial reception, the military terminal organization is sequenced into the AO early enough to conduct timely discharge operations. The planning must provide for the off-loading of MHE equipment to allow for the terminal unit to become operational as soon as possible. Ships should be sequenced into the terminal to match the evolving capabilities of the operating terminal unit. For example, in the early stages of the deployment, RO/RO ships should be scheduled for arrival. Container and other cargo ships should be scheduled only after the terminal has the capability to handle them. However, the transportation planner may consider container off-loading early when using self-sustaining vessels. The availability of HNS also will influence how the ships are scheduled for arrival.

4-72. The terminal unit commander also has planning and execution aspects to consider before off-load operations. Among the aspects, the following are of key importance:

- Coordinating with MSC representatives for ship operations.
- Planning ship discharge and staging.
- Planning for the ship arrival meeting.

- Planning for the provision of ship chandler when there is no MSC presence in the AO.

- Planning to perform harbormaster functions when there is no effective governmental infrastructure to execute this task.

REQUIREMENT FOR PORT SUPPORT ACTIVITIES

4-73. The ASCC normally establishes a requirement for a PSA to meet and assist a deploying unit. This assistance takes place at the SPOD. The PSA may be an advance party from the deploying force or from units in theater. The ASCC and the terminal commander tailor the organization and capabilities of the PSA to the reception or deployment requirements. An agreement between the ASCC and the proper terminal commander defines the PSA support requirements. When the PSA belongs to a deploying force, the ASCC disestablishes it when the parent unit passes through the terminal.

4-74. PSA responsibilities include performing maintenance, providing repair parts, and correcting deficiencies in the equipment shipping configuration. It also provides equipment operators for unique equipment and security for sensitive equipment and classified cargo. The water terminal commander has operational control over the PSA activities. See FM 55-65 for more information on PSA.

WATER TERMINAL DEFENSE REQUIREMENTS

4-75. Water terminals are vulnerable to air and missile attacks, especially if US and allied forces have not established air superiority and sea control. They are also vulnerable to attacks by unconventional forces and to sabotage, terrorism, mining, espionage, and chemical or biological attacks. The rear area security commander includes these threats in the security plan.

INLAND TERMINAL OPERATIONS, PLANNING AND EXECUTION CONSIDERATIONS

4-76. The supported and supporting CINC normally delegates the operation and control of inland terminals to the ASCC, except for Air Force air terminals. The AFSCC has the responsibility for operating the Air Force air terminals.

4-77. The ASCC usually delegates the selection and operation of inland terminals to the senior transportation, aviation, and support command commanders on an area basis. However, their selection requires integrated planning to ensure they link with the LOC and support the concept of operations. These organizations plan for and establish operational inland terminals at both ends of interchange points along the LOC to provide for transshipment of cargo and personnel transported by the modes. The senior transportation commander normally operates transportation inland terminals with cargo transfer companies.

TRUCK TERMINAL AND TRAILER TRANSFER POINT REQUIREMENTS

During Desert Storm, TTPs were used as rest halts and a time to regroup for everyone. Wolf burger mobiles, fuel, and an area for sleeping were some of the capabilities provided by the TTPs.

4-78. The transportation commander places truck terminals in or near centers of concentrated trucking operations at both ends of a line-haul system. He also places TTPs at strategic locations between both ends of a line-haul system.

4-79. Truck terminals connect local pickup and/or delivery service and line-haul operations. They are assembly points and dispatch centers for motor transport equipment used in line-haul operations. They may be used for in-transit storage or freight sorting, but this should normally be minimized as it detracts from efficient operations. Cargo transfer elements provide cargo-handling service at most motor transport terminals.

4-80. The transportation commander may establish one or more intermediate truck terminals at points along the line-haul routes. Their location depends upon the organization of the line-haul operation. The location of supported DS and GS units also influence the selection of sites for intermediate terminals. These terminals provide delivery of cargo to supply support activities. The intermediate terminal may also be collocated with a TTP.

4-81. The transportation commander locates TTPs at predetermined locations along the route of a line-haul operation. They form the connecting links between segments of a route and tie the overall operation into one continuous movement. TTPs offer facilities for exchanging semitrailers between line-haul tractors operating over adjoining segments of a line-haul route. They also provide a means for controlling and reporting equipment engaged in the operation. In specific, TTPs provide facilities for exchanging semitrailers, reporting (ITV), vehicle and cargo inspections, documentation, and dispatch procedures. They may also provide mess, maintenance, and other support. TTPs are not normally used to pick up and deliver cargo.

4-82. Truck terminals and TTPs are established on or as close to the line-haul route as possible. However, requirements for hardstand, support facilities, security, and the availability of real estate may force the establishment of truck terminals or TTPs off of the line-haul route. The truck terminals and TTPs include a marshaling area and other activities and services as required to support the operation. Truck terminal site selectors should consider the following:

- Size, complexity, and duration of the operation.
- Number and type of vehicles to be employed.
- Facilities required at the terminals and transfer points.
- Anticipated backlog of semitrailers at these sites.

RAIL TERMINAL REQUIREMENTS

4-83. Rail terminals include rail yards, freight stations, passenger stations, and repair and service facilities. Except for some rail yards, they are located at the start and the end of rail lines.

4-84. Rail yards are areas with sufficient track lines to allow for the forming of trains. Trains are formed by switching and spotting rail cars. Rail yards are usually available within a rail terminal. However, well developed rail lines usually have one or more rail yards between the start and the end of a line.

4-85. Freight stations are buildings, sheds, or warehouses that provide for receiving, loading, unloading, or storing cargo. A capable freight station enhances the capability to handle cargo. Freight stations usually have a paved access to ease the loading and unloading of other modes of transport. Freight stations also have ramps to ease the handling of tracked and wheeled vehicles. Transportation planners should provide portable ramps to handle tracked and wheeled vehicles anywhere along the rail line.

4-86. Passenger stations contain a track that allows for the spotting of passenger rail cars. They also should include a facility for the use of the troops waiting to board the rail cars. Finally, a rail terminal should have adequate maintenance facilities to repair and service engines and rail cars.

4-87. While Army RC and/or HN rail units operate the railroad, cargo transfer companies operate the terminals. When available and when the tactical situation allows, commanders should exploit rail capabilities within the AO. See FM 55-20 for more information.

INLAND WATERWAY TERMINAL REQUIREMENTS

4-88. An inland waterway terminal normally includes facilities for mooring, cargo loading and unloading, dispatching and controlling, and repairing and servicing all craft capable of navigating the waterway. Appropriate cargo transfer units operate inland waterway terminals. The number of units required depends on the results of an inland waterway terminal throughput analysis.

4-89. Operational level inland waterway terminals along an inland waterway system can be classified as general cargo, container, liquid, or dry bulk commodity terminals. Terminals of the latter three types usually include special loading and discharge equipment that permits efficient handling of large volumes of cargo.

AIR TERMINAL REQUIREMENTS

4-90. Need lead in when this FM is updated.

Air Force Terminals

4-91. The Air Force Component Commander normally provides terminal facilities and operations at all points served by AMC controlled aircraft. Aerial ports are designated for the sustained transshipment of personnel and material and function as air transportation hubs accommodating the loading and unloading of aircraft and in-transit processing of traffic.

4-92. The ASCC may also provide personnel and equipment to participate in loading, unloading, and transshipping Army personnel and material at Air Force operated air terminals. In each of these situations, the ASCC assigns a cargo transfer company or equivalent capability to execute the terminal tasks. The cargo transfer company may also furnish personnel to load and unload Air Force tactical airlift aircraft conducting Army unit moves. The cargo transfer company must accept cargo from the Air Force pending cargo disposition instructions. It may also provide breakbulk facilities for consolidated shipments and cargo awaiting Army transport. The transfer company may also operate a consolidation point for retrograde air shipments. The cargo company is normally attached to the mode operating battalion responsible for clearing cargo from the air terminal.

4-93. Most material delivered by air will be either vehicles or unitized cargo on Air Force 463L pallets. An A/DACG, cargo transfer capable element, or ATMCT will normally be present to coordinate with the TALCE and assist with aircraft off-loading operations. An ATMCT, interacts with the TALCE and the A/DACG (if in place). This team expedites movement of Army personnel and cargo through Air Force and HN air terminals to Army destinations. The ATMCT normally has commitment authority for the onward movement of Army cargo from the air terminal to other terminals, including the final destination. They also coordinate with the line-haul mode operators to assure timely arrival of clearance transports at the air terminal or in-transit area. The ATMCT also coordinates the local movement of retrograde Army material and personnel.

Army Air Terminals

4-94. The ASCC delegates the responsibility for selecting and operating Army air terminals to the senior Aviation commander. Army transportation units provide support as required by establishing a cargo and passenger operation within the Army air terminals as required. The procedures followed when supporting Air Force terminals apply.

SECTION V - Terminal Operations at the Tactical Level of War

INTRODUCTION

4-95. Tactical terminals perform similar functions as the terminals operating at the strategic and operational level. Their main role is to make cargo and personnel accessible to the tactical units. At the Corps, division, and brigade level, transportation systems and tactical terminals provide the key link between dispersed supply units and frequently moving supported units. Tactical terminals enable the logistical system to move supplies, equipment, and personnel on the battlefield in support of the tactical commander's concept of operations. In short, tactical terminal operations afford the commander the capability to concentrate combat power at the critical time and place to influence the battle.

4-96. The biggest challenge is moving ammunition, water, and bulk fuel from Corps rear area to DSAs or BSAs. Terminal operations at this level of war consider the habitual support relationships that exist between truck and transfer elements and ammunition and petroleum supply companies.

ARMY TERMINAL ORGANIZATIONS

4-97. Transportation planners choose from among a variety of Army transportation units to field those necessary to operate the terminals in the tactical AO. These organizations are designed to provide maximum flexibility. They allow a planner to fit the units to the commander's concept of the operation by matching them with the size of the force deployed and the characteristics of the terminals required.

4-98. To provide command and control for the terminal units, the transportation structure provides the COSCOM with the transportation support organizations needed to command and control the terminals. To provide support for a Corps, the Army uses a transportation composite group. When the size of the force is a division or brigade, a transportation battalion may be the senior Army terminal activity in the AO. The elements discussed above may command and control the modes of transport available in the AO in addition to the terminals.

CORPS TERMINAL OPERATIONS, PLANNING AND EXECUTION CONSIDERATIONS

4-99. At the Corps level, the COSCOM functions as the major subordinate command responsible for the direction and management of logistics and terminal operations in the Corps area. Exceptions include operational level supply activities and depots or terminals at inland waterway or rail lines, located within the Corps AO. In these instances, close coordination between the COSCOM and the operational level of war transportation command will provide for the efficient and effective operation of these terminals.

4-100. The tactical commander establishes terminals at Corps Army airfields, depots, supply support activities, or any other suitable location. These terminals permit the loading, unloading, processing, or handling of in-transit personnel and materiel between various transportation modes.

4-101. The COSCOM commander normally attaches a variable number of motor transport, cargo transfer, and trailer transfer units to the subordinate CSGs and battalions to form critical inland terminal links in the theater distribution system. These units may establish truck terminals and TTPs to support the operation. Attachments normally depend on the scope and duration of supported operations, availability of HNS equivalent units, requirements to transport supplies, equipment, and units, and the distribution pattern.

4-102. Theater dependent, the COSCOM can attach a US transportation HN CLT to a CSG. The terminal transfer CLT provides the liaison and interface between the MCC and wartime HNS TTB.

4-103. To support the supply system, transportation personnel need to determine transportation and terminal requirements. Planners must analyze how requirements change as terminal operations support offensive, defensive, and retrograde operations.

AIR FORCE AIR TERMINALS

4-104. The Air Force may establish air terminals in the Corps AO to support theater airlift missions. In these instances, the AFSCC provides terminal operations to load and off-load Air Force aircraft. However, the Army tactical commander may provide personnel to participate in loading and unloading Army personnel and equipment at these facilities. These operations are similar to those executed at Air Force terminals located at the operational level of war. The tactical commander may also accept responsibility for loading and unloading Air Force aircraft at other forward landing fields or airstrips that are not a regularly scheduled stop for theater airlift aircraft. A cargo transfer company may, in each of these situations, execute the terminal mission. The cargo transfer company may furnish personnel to load and unload Air Force theater airlift aircraft conducting Army unit moves. It may provide breakbulk facilities for consolidated shipments and cargo awaiting Army ground transport. The cargo transfer company may also operate a consolidation point for retrograde air shipments. The cargo transfer company is normally attached to the mode operating battalion responsible for clearing cargo from the air terminal.

ARMY AIR TERMINALS

4-105. The Corps aviation brigade operates the Army airfields. The COSCOM operates the air terminals on the Corps Army airfields. Facilities and services are provided at these terminals to support the air movement of personnel and supplies and for the efficient use of available aircraft. The tactical commander may assign cargo transfer units to load and unload aircraft, document cargo, and operate cargo segregation and temporary holding facilities.

DIVISION TERMINAL OPERATIONS, PLANNING AND EXECUTION CONSIDERATIONS

4-106. At the division level, the DISCOM provides for the direction and management of logistics and most terminal operations. Division terminal operations may be difficult to distinguish from organic CSS operations performed by the DISCOM MSB or FSB. At this level, a terminal operation is typically conducted at the DSA, BSA, or other fixed supply or distribution points (general, ammo, petroleum, water, and so on), including forward airfields. Terminals may also be nodes even further forward, such as battalion trains, where individual customers are furnished supplies.

4-107. Tactical terminals at the division level are often the final nodes in the transportation/distribution system. However, equally important, tactical terminals also serve as the origin terminals during redeployment and retrograde operations.

4-108. Terminals at this level are usually characterized by lesser capabilities than at the operational level and may have to be augmented to meet particular phases of the operation or requirements. The key requirement for tactical terminals operated by the DISCOM and other organic CSS units is that flexibility is a must in both operation and location to provide maximum support to the combat commander.

OFFENSIVE OPERATIONS

4-109. Offensive operations often require extended supply lines. Terminals, as the nodes used for final distribution, structure the supply lines. For this reason, the location of the terminals must be planned to coincide with the phases of the attack. The logistic plan must provide for a terminal support structure designed to increase the cargo throughput capability of the entire transportation system.

4-110. Maintaining an adequate stream of support requires the prompt turnaround of transportation assets. Forward delivery of cargo results in large numbers of Corps assets in division areas and division assets in brigade areas. These assets deliver fuel to MSB and FSB class III points and ammunition to ATPs. Efficient terminal operations perform a crucial mission. They provide stability to a system that can often present a confusing picture. They provide the stability by managing the final delivery of cargo and assuring the prompt turnaround of transportation assets.

DEFENSIVE OPERATIONS

4-111. Defensive operations often require shorter supply lines. During these operations, terminal operations involving the handling of fuel decrease. However, terminals handling ammunition normally increase their tempo. Increased loading, unloading, and processing of barrier and fortification materials is also the norm. The right MHE at the right terminal is important, as most of the commodities handled during these operations are heavy.

RETROGRADE OPERATIONS

4-112. Retrograde operations may require the extending of supply lines. Like in offensive operations, the logistic plan must provide for a terminal support structure designed to support cargo movements. The plan should provide for the integration and consolidation of cargo at selected transfer points early in the operation.

4-113. The selection of terminals, to include alternate locations, must support the concept of the operation. This means terminals must have the right supplies to continue to support the tactical operations of the combat units conducting the retrograde operation. Tactical terminals move to new or alternate operational areas at appropriate times.

Chapter 5

Mode Operations

Need lead in when this FM is updated.

INTRODUCTION

5-1. The modes of transport bring to life the Army transportation system. They are the arteries that feed terminals, delivering the deploying force and distributing supplies into and within the AO. The modes give structure to the transportation system, defining the air and surface LOC required to conduct and support a military operation.

SECTION I - Modes of Transport

INTRODUCTION

5-2. There are two transport modes (air and surface) available for the conduct of military operations. The air mode consists of fixed-wing and rotary-wing aircraft. The surface mode includes sea, highway, rail, and pipeline.

5-3. The transport modes used depends on the existing geography and developmental infrastructure available in the AO. The type of military operation and the political nature of the US involvement may also influence mode selection. For example, in a peacekeeping operation, the political arrangements may limit the modes to a designated highway capability.

5-4. Commanders should equip the force with as many mode varieties as possible. A redundancy of modes enhances the flexibility of the transportation system, making it more responsive to changing situations. The parallel use of inland waterway and water transport assets, for example, may allow operations to continue if one MSR is denied due to local conditions.

AIR MODE OF TRANSPORT

5-5. The air mode consists of a variety of assets. These assets include Air Force strategic and theater airlift, as well as commercial fixed-wing assets. The capability also includes Army organic rotary-wing and operational support fixed-wing airlift.

5-6. The Air Force uses its military assets, under the command of AMC, at all levels of war. Commercial air assets are, for the most part, limited to operating at the strategic level of war. Army rotary-wing and operational support airlift work at the operational and tactical levels of war.

5-7. Commercial, US Air Force, and Army operational support airlift assets require an improved base support infrastructure. Army rotary-wing aircraft can operate with a less improved base support structure. Helicopters do not require a paved runway to take-off or land during the conduct of operations.

SURFACE MODES OF TRANSPORT

5-8. Surface modes of transport consists of the following categories:

- Sea.
- Highway.
- Rail.
- Pipeline.

SEA MODE OF TRANSPORT

5-9. The sea mode of transport consists of Navy and Army sealift assets. The Navy assets consist of the active and ROS fleet and those assets acquired from the RRF. The MSC ROS includes assets such as fast sealift ships and prepositioned afloat ships. The RRF includes assets such as RO/RO, container, and bulk POL ships. Commercial shipping organizations may provide assets at the request of USTRANSCOM. These assets work primarily in the strategic level of war transportation system.

5-10. The Army's contribution to the sea mode of transport consists of a variety intracoastal and inland waterways and landing craft. The Army also has amphibians, barges, tugs, and logistics support vessels. The Army uses these assets to work terminals and lighterage operations. The Army uses logistic support vessels to support landings and for intracoastal shipping operations. Army assets work primarily at the operational and tactical levels of war. The ASCC should consider the availability of HNS or contracted assets to supplement the Army capability.

5-11. The use of the sea mode of transport requires the availability or establishment of water terminals. Obtaining viable water terminals may require their early capture. Engineering resources may also enhance existing HN facilities. Army sea transport assets may join Navy and Marine Corps assets to support amphibious assaults and JLOTS operations.

HIGHWAY MODE OF TRANSPORT

5-12. The highway mode of transport consists of a variety of Army truck transportation units that includes commercial assets. In most joint operations, the Army provides the entire highway common-user mode of transport capability. The Army uses this capability to move equipment, supplies, and personnel to POEs where they link with strategic airlift or sealift. The Army also uses highway assets to clear PODs and to distribute the shipments to their destination.

5-13. Commanders should consider the requirements for specialized highway transport capabilities such as water and fuel (POL) tankers, HETS, and PLS. All highway assets support the redeployment of the force.

RAIL MODE OF TRANSPORT

5-14. The Army's capability to operate railways resides within the RCs. However, this capability does not include the equipment needed to mount a railway operation. For this reason, the Army's ability to use rail transport depends largely on the existing capability in the AO.

5-15. Rail is primarily a strategic and operational level of war asset. At the strategic level within CONUS, MTMC arranges for rail movements of cargo and personnel to POE. In OCONUS, the ASCC is responsible for doing the same when deploying an Army force in support of a military operation. At the operational level of war, rail provides onward movement of the force and its sustainment. The Army can use HNS or contracted resources within the AO. The establishment of rail operations requires engineer support to maintain the right-of-ways and terminals.

PIPELINE MODE OF TRANSPORT

5-16. Pipelines allow for the movement of large quantities of bulk petroleum and water. The Army has the capability to lay and operate pipelines. However, commanders should exploit the capabilities existing in the AO. Like rail movements, pipelines require engineering efforts to construct and maintain the pipeline, its pumping stations, and terminals. Quartermaster Corps units operate pipelines primarily at the strategic and operational levels of war.

MODE OF TRANSPORT SELECTION CRITERIA

5-17. Selecting the mode of transport for a particular mission, regardless of the level of war, requires the consideration of certain criteria. The criteria are priority of the requirement, RDD, type of cargo, special restrictions, economy and efficiency, available resources, and security.

PRIORITY OF THE REQUIREMENT

5-18. The priority of the shipment comes from the user and matches the commander's concept of the operation. It is the first and most important consideration. Whenever doubt surfaces regarding the priority of a shipment, authorities in the transportation request process system should ask for validation of the shipment.

REQUIRED DELIVERY DATE

5-19. The RDD should match the priority given to the shipment. The RDD will allow movement control organizations to select the best mode of transportation. The mode operator then selects the assets to deliver the cargo on schedule, considering all the other requirements.

TYPE OF CARGO

5-20. The commodity or type of cargo may dictate which mode to use. Size, weight, packaging, quantity, value, and compatibility are all factors that influence the mode of transport.

SPECIAL RESTRICTIONS

5-21. Special restrictions play an important role not only in the selection of the mode, but in the routing of the movement as well. In coordination with movement control personnel, mode operators must be fully aware of restrictions that may exist along all LOC. These restrictions may dictate the use of a specific mode.

ECONOMY AND EFFICIENCY

5-22. The process of transporting the force and its sustainment is an expensive undertaking. The use of this criteria is important to assure judicious resource utilization. Warning of priority shipments is one method used to assure the sound application of this criteria. With warning, mode operators and the movement control personnel can schedule equipment to match priorities while using the most economical mode of transport.

AVAILABLE RESOURCES

5-23. Mode operators and movement control personnel should maintain a record of used and unused assets. This data is then used as a basis to acquire additional assets.

MODE OF TRANSPORT CAPABILITIES AND LIMITATIONS

5-24. The mode of transport selection criteria must be balanced with the mode capabilities and limitations in order to reach sound decisions. Table 5-1, pages 5-5 through 5-7, describes each mode showing its most effective use, together with capabilities and limitations.

INTERMODAL OPERATIONS

5-25. Intermodal capability is the ability of modes to transfer shipments from one to another with minimum handling requirements. It involves more than the mode of transport; it also includes the container, packaging, or other preparations used to deliver the cargo.

5-26. The positioning of the right MHE at the right location to handle the cargo is very important in intermodal operations. Also crucial is the preparation of cargo ahead of time to guarantee acceptability by the succeeding mode. For example, having the capability to transfer equipment rapidly from sea to air near an SPOE is a function of preparing the equipment to meet Air Force and US Navy loading requirements prior to making the shipment.

Table 5-1. Mode of Transport Capabilities and Limitations

ORDER OF ECONOMY	MOST EFFECTIVE USE	CAPABILITIES	LIMITATIONS
Pipeline	Primary mode for bulk liquids and solids suspended in liquid.	All weather conditions, few terrain restrictions, most economical and reliable mode for bulk liquids, relatively few personnel required for operation and maintenance.	Flexibility limited by immobile facilities, vulnerable to sabotage and enemy action, large construction tonnages required.
Sea	Primary over-ocean mode. Inland surface mode for moving large quantities of cargo.	All weather conditions, any commodity, most economical overall long-distance carrier, particularly useful for relieving other modes to more suitable employment.	Relatively slow, flexibility limited by adequacy of waterways, facilities, and channels, vulnerable to enemy action and difficult to restore. Also, inland waterways subject to flooding and freezing.
Rail	Primary inland mode for sustained flow of large quantities of traffic over long distances.	All weather conditions, any commodity, most economical continuous line-haul operations, greatest sustained ton-mile capability, variety of specialized equipment and services.	Flexibility limited by fixed routes, rail-line clearances restrict outsize movements, capability limited by availability of tractive power, rail-line highly vulnerable to enemy action.

Table 5-1. Mode of Transport Capabilities and Limitations (continued)

ORDER OF ECONOMY	MOST EFFECTIVE USE	CAPABILITIES	LIMITATIONS
Highway	Supplementary mode for making possible an integrated transportation system. Effective in scheduled line-haul operations by the trailer relay system, primary mode for distribution operations and logistical support operations in combat zone.	Most flexible mode over trafficable terrain, practically all weather conditions (terrain factor important), increased flexibility of other modes, can transport nearly any commodity with a variety of specialized equipment for both on- and off-road movement.	Over the road operations affected by route interferences and obstacles created by weather, terrain, or enemy action sustained line-haul operations over long distances uneconomical in terms of ton-mile output versus expenditure of manpower and equipment.
Army Air (Rotary-Wing)	The most costly Army mode for the movement of supplies. Becomes the primary mode of transport when all others are ineffective because of limitations or physical restrictions. Used to move only those high-priority items and critically needed supplies, such as class V, III, I, IX, or as selected by mode managers.	All terrain. Effective over short distances less than 40 km for external loads. Helicopter can use unimproved pickup zone and landing zone during external lift operations. CAPABLE OF LIFTING NEARLY ANY LOAD THAT CAN BE SAFELY RIGGED and that is WITHIN THE WEIGHT limitations of the helicopter. CH-47 helicopters are capable of using Air Force	Operational capabilities limited by weather. Restricted flights in snow conditions and thunderstorms. Freezing levels above surface may limit capabilities. Aircraft capabilities limited by cargo load weight, cargo hook limits, or cargo door sizes. Aircraft availability may be affected by flying hour program or

Table 5-1. Mode of Transport Capabilities and Limitations (continued)

ORDER OF ECONOMY	MOST EFFECTIVE USE	CAPABILITIES	LIMITATIONS
		463L pallets and standard NATO warehouse pallets, when they are equipped with the helicopter internal cargo handling system.	crew rest requirements. Internal cargo loading may require MHE.
Army-Fixed-Wing Army Air Force	Complementary mode for expediting movement of mission essential traffic, primary or major supplementary mode when terrain reduces effectiveness of surface modes, scheduled operation is most economical method of employment and produced greatest sustained ton-mile capability.	Greatest potential speed of delivery, most flexible with respect to terrain obstacles, economically more favorably (when these factors are combined with substantial lift capability and air transport over long distances). Capabilities are: heavy drop, container delivery system, low altitude parachute extraction system, airland, adverse weather aerial delivery system, aerial bulk fuel delivery system.	Requires the availability of airfields. For other limitations see the preceding Army air limitations.

5-27. To optimize the transportation system capacity, the Army uses intermodal systems for contingency and peacetime movements of general cargo, unit equipment, and ammunition. The most common system is the container. It can transfer from highway to rail or sea without disturbing its contents. The Army standard container is the 20-foot, ISO container. However, many commercial containers are also used in the process of supporting a military operation. The most commonly available military useful ISO containers are 20 and 40 feet in length. The main concern when handling containers is the positioning of adequate MHE at the in-transit terminals and an unstuffing capability at the destination terminal. Transportation operators should acquire the required MHE from commercial or HN sources when the organic capability is insufficient to provide adequate resources for all terminals.

5-28. Containers employed in intermodal systems should be returned to the transportation system as soon as feasible. The rapid return of containers will ensure the system is not degraded.

5-29. Another Army intermodal capability is the PLS. PLS enhanced flatracks move, to the maximum extent possible, ammunition basic loads from home stations/depots to SPOEs. PLS enhanced flatracks can also move surge ammunition into the theater when sufficient PLS trucks are available to handle their forward movement.

5-30. Transportation planners and operators should give prime consideration to the intermodality aspects of the deployment of the force. Prepositioning of containers and flatracks at the installation level will optimize the time available for preparation. The distribution plan also provides an answer to how far forward the containers are to go. Ideally, the 40-foot ISO standard containers should go as far as there is a capability to handle them in the AO. PLS flatracks can go as far forward as individual firing batteries.

SECTION II - Mode of Transport Operations at the Strategic Level of War

INTRODUCTION

5-31. Mode of transport operations at the strategic level of war primarily comes under the control of USTRANSCOM. The exception is theater based assets used by supporting CINCs located OCONUS. They exercise this responsibility when deploying a force to a POE in support of another CINC.

5-32. USTRANSCOM oversees the mode operations using its TCCs in coordination with the supported CINC. FORSCOM executes Army mode operations when the deployment originates in CONUS. The ASCC subordinate to the supporting CINC, executes the Army mode operations when the deploying force is OCONUS.

AIR MODE OPERATIONS, PLANNING AND EXECUTION CONSIDERATIONS

5-33. USTRANSCOM uses its strategic airlift assets to support operations through the range of military operations. These assets consist of the C-5, C-141, C-17, KC-10, and KC-135 aircraft in peacetime. Additional strategic airlift is available during contingencies through use of the CRAF. USTRANSCOM may operate channel traffic into areas of operation and manage the traffic much like a commercial airline. USTRANSCOM routinely uses its assets and supplements this capability with commercially contracted aircraft.

5-34. During the execution of a military contingency, USTRANSCOM, through AMC, provides strategic airlift to the supported and supporting CINCs. Strategic airlift normally moves personnel and high priority cargo. The personnel movements are timed so they arrive at their destination sequenced to match the arrival of their equipment. This assures rapid POD clearance as personnel link with their equipment. USTRANSCOM, through AMC, controls the airlift while en route to their destinations.

5-35. Regional combatant commanders usually have, within the AFSCC, an organic fixed-wing capability. This capability consists of C-130 aircraft. The ASCC, by entering the theater airlift request system, may use these assets in a strategic role to transport deploying Army units to POE. Joint Pub 4-01.1 contains more detailed information on the use of Air Force airlift.

5-36. The moving unit or shipper is responsible for preparing the cargo for shipment. This preparation may include airland or airdrop operations. In this regard, the ASCC should make full use of Army organic rigging capability and the A/DACG or other organization designed to assist the deploying unit. The ASCC should coordinate closely with Air Force TALCE.

SURFACE MODE OPERATIONS, PLANNING AND EXECUTION CONSIDERATIONS

5-37. Need lead in when this FM is updated.

SEA

5-38. USTRANSCOM, through MSC, uses organic, activated, or contracted sealift capability. These assets may include fast sealift ships, prepositioned afloat ships, RO/RO, container, or LO/LO ships. USTRANSCOM provides the sealift to support peacetime and crisis oriented military operations. Sealift carries more cargo than any other mode. The supported CINC coordinates the selection of destination water terminals with USTRANSCOM. If the tactical situation changes while the equipment is en route, the CINC may direct the sealift asset be diverted to another water terminal.

5-39. During peacetime operations, movement control organizations offer cargo for sealift shipment through MTMC to MSC. MTMC and MSC coordinate movement from origin to POD. MTMC routinely calls forward and loads the cargo aboard vessels. The priorities and RDDs of the supported command are honored during this process.

5-40. During the execution of a military contingency, USTRANSCOM provides sealift support based on the TPFDL. Sealift may consist of MSC organic or contracted vessels and the prepositioned afloat capability. Fuel and ammunition are moved using dedicated vessels much in the same way as it is done in peacetime, except with more intensity.

5-41. Sealift is also available at the strategic level of war to move unit equipment and sustainment using inland waterways. Barges usually execute this task. Movement by barges is slow and best suited to bulk cargo. USTRANSCOM and supporting CINCs will consider the use of commercial barge carriers to move a military shipment to an SPOE only when time permits. Commercial barge carriers may also be used when other modes are not available.

5-42. The ASCC responsibility, when using sealift, is to prepare the cargo for shipment and provide a PSA, if required. The ASCC should use the DSBs to assist in this process. Close coordination between movement control and installation transportation officers and MTMC is vital. Coordination with the ASCC to obtain the commander's intent prior to loading, assures the proper use of the MSC provided sealift assets. Joint Pub 4-01.2 contains a detailed description of the sealift acquisition process and the type of assets expected to be available to execute a military contingency. See FM 55-65 for preparation of equipment for movement.

HIGHWAY

5-43. USTRANSCOM, through its Army component MTMC, arranges for the use of strategic highway mode assets within CONUS. Supporting CINCs and subordinate ASCC in OCONUS locations have this responsibility when deploying a force from their AO in support of another CINC.

5-44. Within CONUS, MTMC arranges for highway assets required to supplement the capability of the deploying unit. MTMC acquires these assets from the commercial sector using existing tenders of service. They consist of trucks, tractors, trailers, container chassis, and low-bed semitrailers. MTMC also arranges for highway assets to move cargo that requires special handling, such as ammunition. Movement by highway to the APOEs and SPOEs normally occurs when the distance from origin to destination does not exceed a one day drive. If the movement exceeds a one day drive, the equipment moves by rail. MTMC and all supported organizations follow the procedures contained in AR 55-355 through the range of military operations.

5-45. In OCONUS, the ASCC, complying with the priorities of the CINC, uses the organic transportation highway units to move personnel and cargo to the POEs. These units are transportation truck companies containing line-haul and local-haul assets. The ASCC supplements its organic highway capability using HN or contracted support. The ASCC also arranges for highway assets required to handle special shipments such as ammunition and petroleum. The ASCC establishes a time-distance criteria for the use of highway assets within the AO. The ASCC tailors the criteria to the size of the AO, the nature of the operation, and the terrain.

5-46. Because of its door-to-door capability, the highway mode is the most flexible available. It is the best asset to finish an operation because it can link major and intermediate terminals to their final destinations.

RAIL

5-47. USTRANSCOM, through its Army component MTMC, provides rail services within CONUS. Supporting CINCs and subordinate ASCC in OCONUS locations have this responsibility when deploying a force in support of another CINC.

5-48. Within CONUS, USTRANSCOM obtains most of the rail capability from the commercial sector. USTRANSCOM also provides railcars maintained as a part of the DFRIF. These cars, known as "DODX", are the responsibility of MTMC and contain track vehicle bearing capabilities to include tie-down devices. USTRANSCOM arranges for rail movements by spotting railcars at designated installations. This spotting is done in coordination with the ASCC and the ITOs or depot transportation officers.

5-49. Rail is the preferred mode to move track vehicles to APOEs or SPOEs. It is also the most advantageous mode to use for sustained flow of large quantities of traffic over long distances. The ASCC responsibility during rail deployments includes the preparation and loading of the equipment in the sequence required by the priorities established by the supported CINC. The ASCC is also responsible for assuring that Army installations maintain their organic track, loading ramps, and other staging facilities required to support their deployment mission.

5-50. The ASCC also assures the conduct of training for deploying unit personnel. The training includes all the skills needed to load and secure the equipment safely. The ASCC should seek the advice and help from the DSBs to train unit personnel to execute an actual loading operation.

5-51. The commercial rail industry normally requires up to seven days to position large numbers of military useful railcars at installations. To overcome this time lag, the industry in coordination with MTMC, arranges to position or "Spot" military-owned and military-managed strategic railcars near the most likely expected use sites. The deploying unit loads spotted railcars. Required tie-down devices, other than those on board some DFRIF railcars, are provided by the installation supporting the deployment.

5-52. Once loaded, trains are formed and the shipment called forward to match the arrival of the strategic lift asset at the APOE or SPOE. USTRANSCOM and its Army component MTMC, follow the procedures contained in AR 55-355 when arranging rail movements through the range of military operations.

5-53. In OCONUS, the ASCC usually arranges for the use of rail assets through HNS or contract based on the CINCs priorities. The ASCC provides for and tailors its rail planning and execution considerations to local operating conditions.

PIPELINES

5-54. Pipelines at the strategic level of war are the responsibility of DLA. This agency, through the DFSC, its subordinate fuel strategic operator, provides all fuel to the AO. Joint Pub 4-02, contains information concerning the strategic petroleum support operations.

SECTION III - Mode of Transport Operations at the Operational Level of War

INTRODUCTION

5-55. Responsibilities for Army mode transport operations at the operational level of war rests with the ASCC. Depending on the size of the force deployed, the ASCC may have a TRANSCOM, a composite group, a COSCOM, and/or a DISCOM operating the modes.

5-56. The ASCC considers augmenting Corps and division mode of transport capabilities when these organizations execute transportation functions at the operational level of war. The augmentation is tailored to the special requirements of the military operation.

5-57. At this level of war, the Army usually operates the Army air, water, highways, rail, and pipelines to support the military operation. As directed by the CINC, the Army may operate these modes in support of other Services or allied nations. Conversely, at this level of war, the Army is a user in a theater airlift system managed by the AFSCC.

AIR MODE OPERATIONS, PLANNING AND EXECUTION CONSIDERATIONS

5-58. Need lead in when this FM is updated.

AIR FORCE THEATER AIRLIFT SYSTEM

5-59. The ASCC, with its assigned senior transportation commander, coordinates the use of Air Force airlift allocated to the total force. This airlift support consists primarily of C-130 aircraft. The ASCC enters the theater airlift system and follows the request procedures established by the CINC. To facilitate the coordination process, the Air Force assigns a TALO who usually collocates with the appropriate TAMCA, Corps MCC, the DTO, or the element within the task force as designated by the ASCC or tactical commander. Joint Pub 4-01.1 contains detailed information on the conduct of these operations at the operational level of war. FM 55-10 describes Army use of theater airlift.

ARMY AIRLIFT

5-60. Army rotary-wing aircraft at the operational level of war consists primarily of CH-47 helicopters. The ASCC usually retains operational control of these assets. However, some capability is apportioned to appropriate MCCs. The MCCs use this capability to support logistics missions.

5-61. Another capability available at this level of war is the Army operational support airlift assets. The ASCC integrates the use of these assets in moving high priority cargo throughout the AO.

SURFACE MODES OF OPERATION, PLANNING AND EXECUTION CONSIDERATIONS

5-62. Need lead in when this FM is updated.

SEA

5-63. The ASCC, through the senior transportation organization, is responsible for providing operational level of war sealift assets. The nature of the operation and its geographical confines, help the ASCC define the type of assets to use.

5-64. Within the Army force structure, the available assets are landing craft, amphibians, tugs, barges, and logistic support vessels. The ASCC also considers the availability of HNS or contract assets to supplement the Army organic capability. The ASCC uses the assets to mount lighterage operations within a water terminal or through an inland waterways LOC. The ASCC also uses these assets to support intracoastal movements and to establish a LOTS operation.

5-65. When analyzing and assessing the distribution system for an AO, the ASCC determines the requirements for Army sealift type units. Army sealift assets operate mostly in support of water terminal operations. However, they can also execute inland waterway and intracoastal operations. When operating as a carrier of cargo through inland waterways or along a coast, the vessels may cross into areas considered to be the responsibility of the tactical commanders. The ASCC coordinates with the tactical commander to prevent interference with tactical operations and to provide for security. In these instances the responsibility for operating the inland waterways mode capability, to include the terminals, remains with the operational level commander.

5-66. Chapter 3 of FM 55-50 contains the Army planning considerations to use for LOTS operations. Joint Pub 4-06 addresses the joint considerations. Chapter 4 of FM 55-50 contains the considerations to use to establish inland waterways operations. Appendix C contains a summary of Army watercraft organizations showing their capabilities.

HIGHWAY

5-67. The ASCC, through the senior transportation organization, provides the motor transport assets needed to support the operation. These assets range from company to battalion sized units and include a line-haul and often a local-haul capability. The ASCC also considers the availability of contracted or HN specialized truck assets.

5-68. At this level of war, line-haul operations occur between common-user terminals. Local-haul truck assets provide final distribution of supplies and equipment to using organizations. Line-haul truck organizations are located throughout the AO at sites best suited to support the common-user terminals. Local haul assets normally provide assistance to elements of the force located behind the tactical AO.

5-69. The ASCC also considers the requirements for providing specialized truck assets such as HETs, POL, and water tankers. HETs will normally be controlled centrally except when they are in DS of a unit for a specific mission. The POL and water tankers are usually employed on a habitual support basis. The tankers support the supply organizations responsible for providing POL and water within the AO.

5-70. FM 55-30 contains considerations for the establishment of motor transport operations in an AO. Appendix C contains a summary of the capabilities of motor transport units available in the Army force structure.

RAIL

5-71. When available in an AO, the ASCC plans to use this capability. The ASCC may conduct a cost benefit analysis to determine if the use of the rail will provide flexibility by freeing the other modes of transport. The Army force structure for rail operations supplements existing HN rail systems.

5-72. Rail operations may extend into what could be the tactical AOR. In these cases, the responsibility for operating the rail, including the terminals, remains with the operational level ASCC. Transportation staff officers and operators should consider the following factors when planning for the use of a rail operation within the AO.

- The availability of an existing capability.
- The manpower resources available, such as Army force structure, contracted resources, and HNS.
- The state of repair of the rights of way.
- The engineering capability to effect repairs.
- The vulnerability of the rail line.

PIPELINES

5-73. The ASCC may require the establishment of pipelines within the AO. Pipelines usually carry the fuel required to support the force. The ASCC establishes, maintains, and operates the pipelines and terminals. The pipeline operating units execute their mission under guidance received from the JFC JPO. FM 10-1 and FM 10-67 contain considerations to establish pipelines in an AO

SECTION IV - Modes of Transport Operations at the Tactical Level of War

INTRODUCTION

5-74. The modes of transport at the tactical level of war deliver personnel, equipment, and supplies to their final destination. Two modes of transport accomplish this task. These modes are Army air and motor transport (highway). The organizations with these assets are organic to the COSCOM, the Corps aviation brigade, the division aviation brigade, and the DISCOM.

5-75. Aircraft assets include cargo and utility helicopters. Motor transport assets include line-haul and local-haul trucks, and the PLS. Air sorties flown by the Air Force theater airlift organization in the AO may also deliver supplies into units operating at this level of war. Air Force airlift may airland or airdrop to deliver the supplies.

5-76. Although generally restricted to the two modes described above, other modes such as rail, pipelines, and inland waterways may operate at this level. When these modes operate within the tactical level of war, they generally do so under the command and control of the operational level of war transportation elements involved in the military operation.

CORPS MODE OPERATIONS

5-77. Need lead in when this FM is updated.

AIR MODE

5-78. Need lead in when this FM is updated.

Air Force Airlift

5-79. The tactical commander obtains airlift support from the Air Force using the airlift request system established in the AO. The airlift is usually in the form of C-130 aircraft. Within the Corps, three elements participate in this system. They are the Corps G3 and the G4 (who use the CTO) and the MCC. An Air Force liaison officer supports them. Joint Pub 4-01.1 contains a detailed description of the airlift request process.

5-80. The main concern of the tactical commander is the proper use of this asset. It is usually used to deliver high-priority cargo and personnel, sometimes into areas inaccessible by other modes. Planning and coordination are crucial to the employment of these aircraft. Planning involves, but is not limited to, identifying Air Force requirements regarding tie-downs and loading policies and procedures. Coordination with Air Force personnel, ATMCTs, and TALOs is essential prior to the use of the aircraft.

Army Airlift

5-81. The Corps aviation brigade provides Army air assets. These assets are medium and utility helicopters. Helicopters move high-priority cargo and personnel into areas not accessible by any other mode of transport.

5-82. The Corps G3 provides the missions and the priority of support for their use. The G3 coordinates with the Corps G4 to provide for logistics requirements. The G3 allocates air frames to the COSCOM where the MCC enters them in the movement program.

5-83. For special deliveries, such as sling operations, the MCC coordinates the efforts between the aviation brigade elements providing the support and the receiving unit. This coordination includes methods for the return of the slings to the aviation units.

SURFACE MODES

5-84. Need lead in when this FM is updated.

Highway

5-85. Within the Corps, transportation companies may be attached to a transportation battalion or to a Corps support battalion. They are the primary operators of the motor transport capability. These battalions operate under the command and control of the CSG, but respond to the tasking of the MCC. The battalions are organized with light-medium truck companies, medium truck companies, and HET companies. Contracted assets or HN acquired resources are also integrated into the battalions. The truck operations focus on the continuous flow of loaded trucks or semi-trailers from GSUs to DSUs or forward areas. The trucks must be returned expeditiously, loaded with retrograde cargo if possible. Transportation operators consider PLS capability and container handling requirements.

Habitual Support Relationships

5-86. Through use of habitual support relationships, motor transport units perform in DS of commodity oriented supply companies such as ammunition, petroleum, or general supply companies. This allows the drivers to become familiar with the commodities they carry and the locations of the supported elements. It also allows the establishment of hub-and-spoke operations. This relationship parallels the medium truck companies operating in DS of the petroleum supply elements. This concept allows continuous and responsive support, freeing the commander to use logistics to weigh the battle. The concept also allows transportation planners to focus on major Corps redeployments, major changes on distribution patterns, and exception requirements. The execution of this concept may require the reassignment of motor transport elements from one CSG to another in the AO.

Maneuver Unit Relocation

5-87. At times the commander's concept of the operation may require unit relocation within the operational area. The relocation requires placing the necessary motor transport assets in DS of a maneuver commander. HET companies are used to provide relocation support to heavy maneuver units. In these instances, the maneuver commander determines the sequence and priority of the moves.

Task Force Support

5-88. A task force may be formed by the operational level of war commander to execute a special mission. In these cases, motor transport assets are detached to support the task force. The motor transport elements in DS of the task force maintain contact with the MCC to assure the maintenance of a LOC for the duration of the support operation.

Other Surface Modes

5-89. When other surface modes, such as inland waterways and rail, operate in and out of an AO controlled by a tactical level of war commander, the mode operators coordinate the flow of these assets through the AO. The coordination process must include the Corps G3 and other maneuver and fire support units to assure no interference with ongoing military operations. FMs 54-30, 55-30, and 63-3 contain additional information on the use of surface modes of transport in an AO.

DIVISION MODE OPERATIONS

5-90. Need lead in when this FM is updated.

AIR MODE

5-91. Need lead in when this FM is updated.

Air Force Airlift

5-92. A division obtains Air Force airlift support by entering the airlift request system. Within the division, the three key elements involved in this system are the Division G3, Division G4, and the DTO. An Air Force liaison officer collocates with the DTO. Like in the Corps, two processes obtain airlift support. These are the planned request and immediate airlift request processes. Planned requests pass routinely between the requesting unit and the DTO with the assistance of the Air Force liaison officer. Immediate requests require coordination with the G3 and G4 to assure the validation of the requirement. The method of delivery is coordinated with the receiving unit by the MCC. Joint Pub 4-01.1 contains a detailed description of the airlift request process.

Army Airlift

5-93. The division aviation brigade provides Army airlift within the division. The air assets of this brigade are light rotary-wing aircraft. However, the air assault division is equipped with medium rotary-wing aircraft. The brigade responds to commitments and missions received from the G3. The DTO can obtain medium rotary-wing airlift support by contacting the Corps MCC.

SURFACE MODES

5-94. Need lead in when this FM is updated.

Highway

5-95. Within the division, the common-user motor transport company in the MSB of the DISCOM provides support. The organization of this company varies depending on the type division. For example, HETs are organic to this company in a heavy division. The main requirements on this mode of transport are as follows:

- Distributing class I, II, III (packaged), IV, and VII and topographic maps.

- Evacuating tanks and similar pieces of equipment to maintenance collection points (heavy division).

- Transporting division reserve supplies for which the unit is responsible.
- Providing transportation support to displace divisional units that are less than 100 percent mobile.
- Supplementing transportation capabilities of other divisional elements.

The motor transport capability to move ammunition is usually organic to the maneuver and fire support battalions in the division. The division motor transport company supplements this capability when required. The company receives its tasking from the DISCOM MCO.

Other Modes

5-96. Practically every available mode of transport operates in the area controlled by the tactical level of war commander. Examples are Air Force lift airdropping equipment forward and medium lift helicopters from a Corps slinging cargo to forward maneuver or fire support elements. These modes, unless operating in DS of the division, will operate under the operational control of their command and control elements. They function at the operational level of war or at the higher tactical level. The DTO is responsible for coordinating the movement of these modes when they are functioning at the division tactical level of war. FM 55-2 describes mode operations within a division area.

Appendix A

Total Asset Visibility

Need lead in when this FM is updated.

IN-TRANSIT VISIBILITY, COMMUNICATIONS SUPPORT, AND AUTOMATIC IDENTIFICATION TECHNOLOGY

A-1. The DTAV plan, established in April 1992, provides a phased implementation of key policies, procedures, systems, and related communications technologies required by operators and logisticians for essential visibility of DOD materiel assets. The DTAV concept uses many existing systems and commercial "off-the-shelf" software to track the location, quantity, and condition of selected major end items, reparables, ammunition, and other support items.

A-2. The concept of TAV originates from a larger DOD initiative known as the IRP. As one of the encompassing logistical processes, the IRP involves downsizing materiel inventories while maintaining materiel readiness and combat sustainability. To be successful, DTAV must provide users with the aggregate logistical visibility needed to conduct operational and maintenance planning. In meeting this requirement, the DTAV plan has been developed to effectively integrate and focus management and resources on those key visibility requirements that have the greatest potential to improve operational support and reduce inventory levels.

IN-TRANSIT VISIBILITY

A-3. ITV is the capability, through the range of military operations, to identify and track the movement of defense cargo, passengers, medical patients, and personal property from origin to final destination. As a key component of the DTAV plan, ITV plays a large role in providing updated information to enhance the logistics support in wartime, contingencies, and peacetime. Workable efforts such as these will constitute the management of timely and accurate logistical information (for example, visibility over in-storage; in-process; and in-transit) on specific commodities from cradle to grave.

A-4. The conceptual automated process leading to this capability consists of gathering and maintaining timely and accurate source movement data. The timeliness and accuracy of data within management systems depends on the communications systems used to convey the data throughout the system and the frequency with which the data must be re-entered into the system. Ideally, data should be entered once into the system and then perpetuated throughout the automation continuum via the communication system.

A-5. The first and foremost technological component required to enhance ITV within the Army is a seamless automated management system, including assured communications which supports transportation functions from origin to destination.

A-6. The GTN system is being fielded to support and integrate DOD ITV capability. Although presently not fully operational, the GTN's success and continued development are dependent on accurate source movement information provided through the many automated transportation information systems in development or already operational. Other initiatives of importance to the GTN development and ITV capability include the fielding of Service transportation automated information systems, implementing electronic data interchange standards and conventions, developing a communications network to link DOD shippers and commercial carriers, modifying transportation procedures, and introducing automatic identification technologies into the transportation automation continuum.

A-7. USTRANSCOM serves as the DOD functional proponent for the GTN and the ITV portion of the overall DTAV program. Responsibility includes providing the functional oversight, guidance, architecture, and standards needed to develop an integrated and interoperable ITV capability for DOD.

GLOBAL TRANSPORTATION NETWORK

A-8. The GTN, an automated data and communication platform, provides the centralized capability to gather and maintain timely and accurate movement data. The GTN incorporates the best methods, information, and technology available to the DOD and the commercial industry. The source movement data is captured through a broad DOD network of automated information systems. As movement data is captured and stored, the GTN provides worldwide customers access allowing inquiries on in-transit cargo and passengers. Users can query through parameters such as requisition number, national stock number, transportation control number, or social security number. The scope of the GTN, which was initially limited to the transportation systems and networks under the control of USTRANSCOM is evolving to include systems operated by the theater commanders and Services. This provides ITV from origin to final destination transportation activity during peace or war.

A-9. Current visibility capabilities (via GTN) include an air module providing visibility on cargo and passengers from APOE to APOD. It also includes a sealift module providing visibility over surface cargo movements between water ports.

A-10. The present source systems for the air module are the PRAMS, the CAPS II, and the GDSS. The sealift module derives its data from the Mechanized Export Tracking System II, Terminal Management On-Line System, and WPS. The air and sealift modules rely on DLA's DAAS for requisition information. This aggregated data provides the status of requisitions and ITV for passengers and cargo moved on USTRANSCOM component commands' organic, controlled, and charter air and sealift. The capabilities are being designed into the GTN and the applicable subsystems that will be involved.

COMPUTERIZED MOVEMENT PLANNING AND STATUS SYSTEM

A-11. The COMPASS is a FORSCOM unique system designed to meet Army unit movement planning requirements in support of force deployment for joint operations. The COMPASS receives UMD from Active and Reserve Component units, updates joint planning systems (for example, JOPES), and provides transportation related information for mobilization and deployment. The COMPASS is used to maintain the DA standard Equipment Characteristics Data (TB 55-46-1 and the TC-ACCIS ECR) and the DA TUCHA for joint planning purposes.

PRESENT GLOBAL TRANSPORTATION NETWORK SOURCE SYSTEMS

A-12. Need lead in when this FM is updated.

Department of the Army Movement Management System-Redesign

A-13. The DAMMS-R serves as an efficient management information system. It provides a reliable automated information processing capability for planning, programming, coordinating, and controlling movements and transportation resources in a theater of operations during peacetime and wartime. System functions support the readiness mission in garrison and during training exercises to promote the rapid transition to war. DAMMS-R is the standard wartime transportation system for use from TA to separate brigade or ACR level. It provides the TAMCA with a reliable automated capability to support cargo movements, mode asset management, and ITV. It enhances planning, programming, coordination of movements, and control of transportation resources in garrison, during training, and during transition to war. DAMMS-R provides transportation managers the ability to plan, program, and monitor the movement of troops and materiel throughout the theater of operations. DAMMS-R supports the operational and management functions of each echelon of the theater of operation transportation system. It is operated by organizational personnel in a garrison and/or field environment during peacetime, wartime, or OOTW.

A-14. The operational concept for DAMMS-R emphasizes standardized integrated transportation application modules. DAMMS-R operates on standard military tactical computers or comparable nondevelopmental item computers. DAMMS-R, as part of the CSS battlefield functional area control system, is supported by existing peacetime local and long-haul communications systems including the DDN.

A-15. DAMMS-R has seven subsystems. These subsystems include the following:

- Shipment management module.
- MCT operations.
- Transportation addressing subsystem.
- Highway regulation.
- Convoy planning.
- Operational movement programming.
- Mode operations.

A-16. In addition, DAMMS-R will interface with a wide variety of external supply and transportation management information systems. These systems include:

- Cargo Movement Operations System.
- Combat Service Support Control System.
- Global Transportation System.
- Logistics Intelligence File.
- Medical Supply Module of the Theater Army Medical Management Information System.
- Prisoner of War Information System - 2.
- Standard Army Ammunition System.
- Standard Army Retail Supply System - 1.
- Standard Army Retail Supply System - 1, Interim.
- Standard Army Retail Supply System - 2A.
- TC-ACCIS.
- Unit Level Logistics System - Ground.
- Unit Level Logistics System - S4.
- WPS.

The Passenger Reservation and Manifesting System

A-17. The PRAMS is an AMC system that records nonunit passenger reservations, issues boarding passes, and generates the aircraft manifest for fixed AMC APOEs.

The Consolidated Aerial Port System II

A-18. AMC's CAPS II is an umbrella system that includes cargo, passenger, and command and control operations. It provides a standardized worldwide automated network of computers for processing cargo and passengers through the major aerial ports. The cargo system records receipts, staging, and unloading at APOEs, and prints out the aircraft manifest upon completion of loading. The passenger system will accomplish passenger processing, seat allocation, cash collection, flight update processing to ASIFICS/PRAMS, boarding pass, and final manifest preparation/issue.

The Global Decision Support System

A-19. The GDSS records and displays airlift schedules, aircraft arrivals and departures, and aircraft status. It provides executive level decision support and is AMC's primary command and control system. It will be the source of planned and actual itineraries and scheduled allocations for all AMC carriers and tankers. The ADANS is also used to schedule airlift missions (including planned cargo allocation) and will provide schedule/allocation data to the GTN via GDSS.

Terminal Management On-Line System

A-20. This system provides the GTN information about MTMC water terminal operations and cargo accountability. This includes cargo status, planned and actual cargo manifests, location, and disposition information.

Mechanized Export Tracking System II

A-21. MTMC's Mechanized Export Tracking System II will provide the GTN information about surface traffic cargo booking. This includes cargo description and characteristics, status, location, and disposition information.

Worldwide Port System

A-22. The WPS records cargo arrival in a MTMC operated port, staging and outloading cargo. The manifest for ships and appropriate documentation for land movement will also be generated. WPS replaced the DASPS-E, the Terminal Management On-Line Systems TSM, and other MTMC Terminal Support Systems for a fully integrated and standardized Port Operating Support System.

Defense Automated Addressing System

A-23. The DLA's DAAS is the central repository for order status of MILSTRIP transactions between retail and wholesale supply activities.

FUTURE GLOBAL TRANSPORTATION NETWORK SOURCE SYSTEMS

A-24. Additional segments to the transportation pipeline (such as theater and CONUS) and other categories (such as medical patients and personal property) are projected to eventually be embedded into the GTN operational system.

Integrated Booking System

A-25. The IBS will be the unit movement/nonunit resupply traffic management system at MTMC area commands and OCONUS. It will register cargo for sealift, book cargo with ocean carriers, provide schedules for unit arrival at ports, issue port calls to units, and export traffic releases to nonunit resupply cargo. The functions of the METS and the ASPUR will be replaced by the IBS.

CONUS Freight Management System.

A-26. MTMC's CONUS Freight Management System, automates CONUS freight movement and provides a DOD-wide centralized automated information system for the procurement of commercial freight transportation services from "fort to port" in peace and war. Emphasis is on service, economy, and readiness. The CONUS Freight Management System interfaces with multiple DOD transportation, logistics, supply, and financial systems. The interface provides capabilities including cost, carrier selection, movement documentation, prepayment audits, and visibility for shipments of all sizes and weight.

Headquarters On-Line System for Transportation. The

A-27. Headquarters On-Line System for Transportation provides a centralized record of cargo movement requirements to HQ AMC and provides information about air cargo manifests, locations, and status.

Defense Transportation Tracking System.

A-28. The DTTS will provide the GTN information about surface shipments requiring increased surveillance and security while in-transit from CONUS consignor to CONUS consignee.

Integrated Command, Control, and Communications System.

A-29. MSC's IC3 will pass scheduled and actual departure/arrival information, itineraries, and diversions/delays covering sea assets and traffic.

Transportation Coordinators-Automated Information for Movements System.

A-30. The TC-AIMS is the generic term for the Joint Deployment Community's Transportation Automated Command and Control System. TC-AIMS systems are used by transportation coordinators to automate the processes of planning, organizing, coordinating, and controlling unit-related deployment activities supporting the overall deployment process. The Army's TC-ACCIS, already operating, provides ITOs and other movement control organizations the following:

- Unit equipment.
- List data.
- Movement requirements.
- Replies to movement requirements.
- Airlift requests (intratheater).
- Airlift mission schedules.
- File update data.
- Movement event reports.
- Air manifests.
- Passenger manifests.
- Rail load plan data.

USTRANSCOM's Regulating and Command and Control Evacuation System.

A-31. USTRANSCOM's Regulating and Command and Control Evacuation System will integrate the separate processes of medical regulating and aeromedical evacuation, integrating CONUS and separate geographical theaters into a single global system. It will operate with three major groups of information: patient movement requirements; receiving hospital capability; and transportation capability to move patients and provide, by-name, ITV.

GLOBAL COMMAND AND CONTROL SYSTEM

A-32. The GCCS will replace WWMCCS for TPFDD documentation and event reporting. The JPEC will use the GCCS to document movement requirements, transportation closures, and other significant events.

AUTOMATIC IDENTIFICATION TECHNOLOGY

A-33. AIT is a developing concept for employing sophisticated identification technologies to achieve ITV of deployment and distribution operations. It is a means of affixing a technical application (for example, radio frequency tag; microcircuit tag; or bar code) containing movement information to a container or pallet. In this usage, "automatic" refers to the fact that a single entry or retrieval event can result in the capture of a stream of data (from a single character to many thousands). A human operator may or may not be part of the actual entry/retrieval event.

A-34. AIT devices have the capability to store data (transportation, maintenance, and/or supply) permitting rapid and accurate acquisition, retention, and retrieval of source data via several technologies such as radio frequency, contact, or bar scan. Automatic identification includes a spectrum of capabilities including bar coding, microcircuit devices (radio frequency identification) and other sophisticated means of identification. Radio frequency identification, as an example, uses the concept of radio wave transmission and reception to pass information about containers or rolling stock that need to be identified or tracked.

A-35. The information is stored on a device, sometimes referred to as "RF tag," with media storage capability similar to a computer floppy disk. Hand-held or fixed RF interrogators can read the information contained on the RF tag attached to the item and pass it back to a central database. The RF interrogator can also electronically write to the RF tag in order to update information concerning the "tagged" item. It is this remote read/write capability that sets the radio frequency hardware apart from other automatic identification technologies such as LOGMARS.

A-36. USTRANSCOM, Services, and agencies are testing and evaluating AIT applications for containerized/palletized shipments. Based upon application assessments, USTRANSCOM will recommend an AIT standard to the OSD.

Appendix B

Checklist for Establishing a Transportation System

The following checklist covers key considerations for commanders to use when planning and executing Army transportation operations. Inherent to the list, is the abbreviated process that permits the DTS to function effectively during periods of national crisis or war. This checklist will assist commanders and their staff transportation planners and operators, at all levels of war, in establishing an effective transportation system to support the committed Army forces.

Section I highlights planning and execution considerations for senior transportation planners responsible for effectively mobilizing and deploying the force to an AO at the strategic level of war. Section II lists operational and tactical levels of war transportation considerations that must be addressed by transportation planners responsible for the reception, onward movement, and sustainment of the deploying force. Section III lists key considerations that should be addressed during the development and execution of a theater movement program.

SECTION I - Strategic Transportation

1. What is the CINC's/JTF commander's concept of operation and the J-4's concept of support?

2. Are these concepts transportation supportable? Is there sufficient transportation capability included in the proposed force structure or available through other means? What means will be used to resolve shortfalls or prioritize use?

3. Will the Army provide common-user transportation support to the other service components? What is the requirement? What will be the impact on support to Army forces?

4. Will the CINC establish a JMC? What is the JMC's scope of authority? Will the Army component have to provide staff augmentation or liaison to the JMC?

5. Is there multinational participation in the operation? Has the US been assigned lead nation logistics responsibilities? Will the Army provide common-user transportation support to other national forces? What is the scope of support? What are the control mechanisms? Who coordinates support and priorities? Is multinational movement control required?

6. Is there a transportation supportable TPFDD? What is the allocation of strategic lift in terms of quantity, type, and frequency?

7. Will the capacities of theater transportation meet or exceed the capacities of strategic lift? If not, how will backlogs be handled?

8. How and when are transportation units phased? Does this phasing support theater transportation requirements? Will sufficient transportation forces introduced early enough to open ports and provide onward movement based on the programmed arrival of forces?

9. If there are multinational forces, is there a combined TPFDD? What control mechanisms will deconflict force arrivals at the PODs?

10. Have the capabilities of all ports and LOCs been analyzed? What are the shortfalls? What can be done to increase throughput?

11. What unified commands will provide support (forces/capabilities)? What coordinating mechanisms need to be established for this support?

12. Who will control each LOC? Have responsibilities been assigned?

13. How will in-transit visibility be maintained? What systems are available? What additional support is required?

14. How will sustainment flow? What control mechanisms will be established to ensure the highest priority cargo moves if the system becomes saturated?

15. Have port operators been identified? Have they been provided solid workload estimates from which to plan operating capability?

16. Will prepositioned (Army Reserve) material be used? Has it been incorporated as part of the reception and onward movement plan?

17. What will be security and engineering requirements for transportation nodes? Are any improvements required? Have they been incorporated in staff planning? Has responsibility been assigned?

18. What are the funding guidelines? Is local contracting required?

SECTION II - Operational and Tactical Transportation

GENERAL

1. Is the CINC's/ASCC's strategic theater campaign plan and/or OPLAN provided to assist the implementer?

2. Are the necessary maps for implementing the plan listed available?

3. Is there a concise CINC/ASCC concept of support provided?

4. Does the plan describe how transportation support is to be provided?

5. Have the terrain and enemy intelligence been analyzed to determine the impact on transportation support?

6. What are the facility requirements to support the transportation system? Have these requirements been incorporated in engineer plans? Can any of the facility requirements be satisfied by HN facilities?

7. Is site preparation required?

8. Is there a combined TPFDL provided? Is it transportation supportable? Has it been properly analyzed to determine time-phasing for introduction of transportation elements?

9. Has HNS transportation availability and risk been considered?

10. Who is the contracting authority in theater?

11. Will units/sustainment flow through an ISB? Where are the ISBs? Who operates the ISBs?

12. Is there a requirement for area oriented depots to arrange for special assignment airlift mission to expedite cargo distribution to the AO?

13. Are the transportation support systems for direct support system and air LOC described?

14. Is coastal LOC required (Army freight ships, landing craft, lighterage)?

15. Are there coastal restrictions?

16. Is a LOTS operation required?

17. Have MHE requirements been addressed?

18. Are in-country highway, rail, air, and inland waterway mode requirements addressed?

19. What ports are available? What is access to or from the ports? What special port clearance requirements apply?

20. Is transportation movement priority provided?

21. What is the weather impact on ports, airfields, and highway nets?

22. What is the availability of Defense Intelligence Agency data or analysis regarding the country or area transportation infrastructure?

23. What are the transportation funding arrangements?

24. Are transportation account code requirements specified?

25. Are the SPOD/SPOE and APOD/APOE specified?

26. Has the use of foreign flag sea or airlift been addressed?

27. Is an intratheater, intertheater, and in-country movement system for personnel and cargo specified?

28. Are procedures for shipping supplies and equipment that arrive at the home station after units have deployed addressed?

29. Have medical evacuation requirements been included in the plan?

30. Is refrigerated transportation required?

31. What support is provided by the HN, allies, or other Services?

32. Is pipeline capability present? How much? Who is the operator?

33. Are retrograde procedures spelled out for excess and unserviceable items?

34. Are there provisions in the plan for maneuver/war damage resulting from transportation operations?

35. Are special Department of Agriculture and US Public Health Service cleaning requirements for retrograde equipment identified?

36. What are diplomatic and technical clearance requirements for movement through other countries?

RECEPTION AND ONWARD MOVEMENT

1. What elements are being airlifted?

2. What elements are being sealifted?

3. What is the time-phasing of initial transportation capability into the area of operation (for example, port opening packages and MCTs)?

4. How much transportation support is provided by the joint task force?

5. Does the joint force require any common-user transportation support from the Army?

6. Are movements of personnel, equipment, and supplies included? Have adequate provisions been made for defense during movements?

7. What is the concept of operation for petroleum support of transportation units?

8. Have arrangements been made for the transportation of ammunition within the theater?

9. What is the distribution requirement?

- Are unit and support locations identified?
- Has a distribution pattern been established?
- Are transportation units programmed to arrive at locations that support the distribution pattern?
- Are there tonnage estimates?
- Have these been balanced against unit requirements?
- Is there a plan to distribute pre-positioned material?

MOVEMENT CONTROL

1. What is the CINC's/ASCC's concept for movement control?

2. When do movement control elements arrive?

3. Has an individual component commander been given responsibility for theater movement control? Has it been coordinated with other component commanders?

4. Has each component been given the responsibility for its own movement control?

5. Have joint-use transportation requirements been established?

6. Has a JTB been established?

7. Has a JMC been established to ensure transportation requests are validated and theater common-user transportation resources are employed with maximum effectiveness?

8. What are the theater common-user transportation requirements and capabilities?

9. What HN transportation facilities and equipment are available?

10. Has JMC communications with JOPES been established to monitor and effect changes to the deployment of forces and supplies?

11. What automated transportation systems are available to support TAV and ITV?

12. Has a TAMCA been established?

13. Is there an MCC?

14. How many Movement Control organizations are assigned and where?

15. How many MCTs are assigned and where?

16. Has Army airlift been allocated for logistics purposes?

TERMINAL OPERATIONS
GENERAL

1. What terminal facilities are available, including ports, airfields, rail, and inland waterways? Have appropriate surveys been conducted?

2. For whom do terminal operators work?

3. Are tonnage forecasts available?

4. What type and number of terminal transfer units are required (rail, highway, port, and/or airfield)? What transportation units are required to support the operation? Who will operate each terminal?

5. Can ammunition be stored at each terminal? How much?

6. Who will provide air traffic control/ harbormaster duties at each POD?

7. Are there hazardous materials restrictions at any terminal?

8. What are the local customs requirements?

9. Is sufficient MHE available?

10. Is sufficient blocking, bracing, and packing material available?

11. Are sufficient facilities available for source mail?

FIXED PORTS

1. What fixed ports are available to support military marine terminal operations?

2. Is a port opening package required? What assets are required?

3. What is the draft of the port?

4. What type and quantities of MHE are available for use in support of military marine terminal operations?

5. How many berths and anchorages are available for use in support of military marine terminal operations?

6. What is the enemy's capability to interdict the ports?

7. What port security measures are currently in use?

8. What is the port's capability to handle containerized cargo and RO/RO cargo?

9. What routes access the ports? Are there any special port clearance requirements?

10. What inland waterways access the port?

11. What is the current throughput capability of the port?

12. What are the characteristics and capabilities of the port's warehouse facilities and storage area? What effect does weather and sea have on port operations?

13. What contract civilian/HN marine terminal personnel and equipment assets are available to support military terminal operations?

14. What is the present level of use of the ports?

15. What capability do government/local civilian contractors have to repair damage to port facilities?

16. What is the ammunition handling capability?

17. What is the heavy lift capability?

LOTS OPERATIONS

1. What shorelines are conducive for LOTS operations?

2. What types of roads access the shorelines?

3. What types of railroads access the shorelines?

4. What civilian contract or HN personnel and equipment assets are available to assist in LOTS operations?

5. What are the predominant weather conditions in the AO?

6. How much engineering support will be required to properly execute a LOTS?

7. What type of LOTS equipment will be required (for example, landing craft; cranes; barges; and so on)?

AIR TERMINALS

1. What airfields can be used? What are their capabilities?

2. Have A/DACG and/or ATMCT requirements been satisfied?

3. Are prerigged projects available for on-call delivery? Are call forward procedures specified? Is airdrop resupply capability provided commensurate with the expected requirement?

4. What are the personnel and cargo reception capabilities of the airfield?

5. What is the current use of the airfield?

6. What are the characteristics and capabilities of the roads that access the airfield?

7. What contract civilian/HN personnel and equipment assets are available to assist in A/DACG operations?

8. What airfield facilities are available for military use during operations?

9. What impact does weather have on airfield operations?

10. What engineer assets are available to upgrade and maintain airfields?

11. Have AMC channel airlift requirements been specified?

12. Has support been planned for US Air Force mobile aeromedical staging facilities?

13. Has a coordinating HQ been designated for all logistical airlift support?

CONTAINER TERMINALS

1. What is the container policy? How far forward are the containers going to go? Is there container handling equipment at all destinations?

2. What civilian contract or HN personnel and equipment assets are available to assist intermodal operations?

3. What is the capability of units and ports to handle container shipments?

4. Can containers be used with carrier delivery direct to the supply support activity?

5. Will other than 20-foot and 40-foot containers be used?

MODE OPERATIONS

HIGHWAY

1. What truck units will support the area of operation?

2. From where do they plan to support?

3. What are their capabilities?

4. Have requirements been balanced against their capabilities?

5. Are truck unit types matched against terrain capabilities?

6. Is the highway net described? What are its capabilities and limitations?

7. What routes are available to support military operations?

8. What are the characteristics and capabilities of the routes available to support military operations?

9. What are the convoy restrictions?

10. What are the dimensions of tunnels along the routes?

11. What are the dimensions and classifications of bridges along the routes?

12. What capability does the government have to repair damaged segments of routes?

13. What engineer assets are available to maintain or upgrade routes?

14. What segments of the routes are heavily used by the civilian populace?

15. What are the most likely routes fleeing refugees might use?

16. What is the best source for additional information on the routes?

RAIL

1. Is there a rail system available?

2. What rail lines are available to support military operations? Who coordinates, who guards, and who pays?

3. What is the condition of the rail lines? What are their schedules and capabilities?

4. What is the gauge of the tracks?

5. What effect does the weather have on rail operations?

6. What rail assets are available to support military operations?

7. Are loading ramps available at rail yards and terminals?

8. What is the location and lifting capacity of railway cranes in the AO?

9. What is the enemy's ability to interdict the rail lines?

10. What capabilities do the government or local civilian contractors have to repair damaged track, bridges, and tunnels?

11. What are the characteristics and capabilities of the rail terminals and marshaling yard?

12. What is the present level of use of the rail lines?

13. What is the description (model number, wheel arrangement, horsepower, weight, tractive effort, and type coupler) of typical line-haul locomotives and switch engines currently in service in the AO?

14. What are the capacities, dimensions (length), and age of typical rolling stock currently in service in the AO?

15. Is a track profile of the main line indicating the location, percent, and length of ruling grade available? Is a plan showing location and length of minimum radius curves together with any sections of multiple main line track available?

16. What are the location and length of passing tracks on the main line?

17. What is the current level of traffic (trains per day) using the main line in the AO?

18. What are the location, type, and capacity of rail yards in the AO?

19. What are the number and length of track in each yard?

20. What are the location; description (type, construction, length, clearances, and Cooper rating); and condition of rail bridges and tunnels on the main line?

21. What are the location, description, and condition of station facilities supporting the operation of the main line?

22. What are the location, storage capacity, and condition of locomotive fueling facilities in the AO?

23. What are the location, capacity, and condition of engine houses and car repair shop facilities in the AO?

24. What are the location and quality of water supply on the main line?

25. What communications and signals are in use for train operations?

26. What is the weight (pounds/yard) of main line rail?

27. What is the predominant type of cross tie used in the AO?

28. What are the location and availability of spare parts for motive power and rolling stock?

29. What type of wheel bearing is used on rolling stock?

INLAND WATERWAYS

1. What inland waterways are available?

2. What are the capabilities and limitations of the inland waterways?

3. What inland terminals are along the waterways?

4. What are the characteristics and capabilities of the inland terminals?

5. What is the present use of the inland waterways?

6. What is the enemy's capability to interdict the inland waterways?

7. What effect does the weather have on the inland waterways?

8. How accessible are the inland waterways to roads and rail lines?

9. What intercoastal shipping assets have been identified to support shipping bulk fuels, ammunition, and dry cargo? Are they available?

10. What intercoastal shipping routes are currently in use?

11. What is the enemy's ability to interdict intercoastal shipping?

SECTION III - The Movement Program

1. Has the distribution pattern been analyzed?

- What is the commander's concept of operation?
- How many incoming units?
- What types of incoming units?
- What is the location of in place units?
- What will be the location of arriving units?
- When will incoming units arrive?
- What is the throughput transportation requirement?
- What is the interzonal transportation requirement?

2. Has the transportation network been developed?

- What intelligence information is available?

- What engineer data is available regarding the transportation network?

- Has mission, enemy, terrain, troops, and time been evaluated?

- Have the locations of mode operators been assigned?

- Have the locations of terminals been assigned?

- Has the receiving, loading, and handling capabilities of shippers and receivers been determined?

3. Have the requirements for the transportation/distribution plan been determined?

- Have shipping forecasts been analyzed?

- Has the supply class, estimated weight, cube, and the RDD been analyzed?

- Is there special handling required?

- Have personnel movement requirements (for example, troops; civilians; patients; and prisoners of war) been assessed?.

- Are there any major subordinate command transportation requirements exceeding organic capability?

4. Have the mode operator capabilities been determined?

- What number, types, and equipment are available?

- Are HN transportation assets available?

- Are third country and US-contracted transportation assets available?

- What reception, material handling, and in-transit storage capability is available?

- Is there an intratheater US airlift/ airdrop capability?

5. Have requirements been balanced against capabilities?

- Have command relationships and geographic AOR been considered?

- Have workload requirements such as the following been considered?

  - Direct shipments.

  - Multistops.

  - Retrograde.

  - Intermodal shipments.

- Are there any transportation shortfalls?

- Where are the critical points in the system?

- Are MCTs assigned to the critical points?

- Has execution been adjusted in accordance with the CINC's priorities and transportation priority of shipments?

- Have adjustments been coordinated with appropriate shippers, receivers, material managers, and logistics staffs?
- Has the requirements schematic been completed?
- Has the mode schematic been completed?
- Have modes been allocated for each shipping requirement?

6. Has the movements program been coordinated and published?

- Has the movement program been fully coordinated with other command movement planners?
- Has the movement program been coordinated with operations, supply, MP, and engineer staffs?
- Has the movement program been approved by the appropriate authority?
- Does the movement program have the appropriate classification?
- Has the movement program been published and distributed to appropriate officials?

Appendix C

Army Transportation Units

This appendix portrays the different types of transportation involved in moving the force. However, the movement function goes well beyond the physical movement of personnel and materiel. It involves all the elements of moving forces and their logistics requirements. Some of the components of movements are the physical transportation modes and the process of planning and controlling movements. The allocation of movement assets is also a critical concern.

The annexes in this appendix depicts those Army organizations involved with moving personnel and materiel through the operational and tactical levels of war.

TOE are programmed to receive a cyclic review and updated every three years. In keeping with the program to continually update TOE, the Transportation Corps is developing new concepts for rail, movement control, and terminal operations. For example, staffing for a new rail concept with a different company makeup. A new cargo transfer company will replace existing cargo transfer companies and terminal service companies.

Transportation Command and Control Units

Need lead in when this FM is updated.

HHC, TRANSCOM (TOE 55601L0000)
MISSION AND ASSIGNMENT

C-A-1. To command, control, and provide technical supervision of assigned/attached units supporting the TA modes of transportation and related services including DS/GS maintenance for rail and Army watercraft. It also provides staff assistance to the TA DCSLOG for theater level transportation plans, policies, and procedures; information on transportation capacity and capability to the TAMCA; liaison with other US and allied forces; and control of designated wartime HNS resources. This unit is assigned to the TA.

CAPABILITIES

C-A-2. Commands and supervises the activities of all transportation HQ and other assigned or attached units operating and/or supporting the TA transportation services required in support of the TA.

FUNCTIONS

C-A-3. Performs the following functions:

- Provides staff planning and coordination of transportation combat services support activities as assigned by the TA DCSLOG.
- Conducts liaison with other US forces, TA, and host and allied nations as directed by the TA DCSLOG.
- Controls, through its subordinate HQ, the HN resources allocated to the TA transportation service.

HHC, TRANSPORTATION COMPOSITE GROUP (TOE 55622L000)
MISSION AND ASSIGNMENT

C-A-4. To command units that provide transportation services for an independent division-sized force, for a two-division separate Corps force, or on an area basis in support of a larger force. This unit is normally assigned to the HQ commanding an independent division-sized force to the Corps, with attachment to the COSCOM, when supporting a two-division separate Corps force; or to a TA, with attachment to a TRANSCOM, when providing support to a larger force.

CAPABILITIES

C-A-5. This unit has the following capabilities:

- Commands, controls, and technically supervises three to seven battalions and their assigned/attached units.

- Develops and supervises implementation of programs, plans, and policies for employment of attached units and contract/ wartime HN agencies/units providing transportation support.

- Provides a liaison officer to its HQ of attachment.

- Provides a nucleus organization during the early stages of the buildup of an immature theater for the development of a transportation brigade or TRANSCOM as the theater matures.

- Performs relational database management and table maintenance functions for the regional segment of the worldwide port system and provides technical supervision of worldwide port system operations throughout the composite group's operational area.

- Coordinates rear area security and damage control activities of subordinate units with the designated rear area commander.

- Commands motor/rail transport; terminal service/cargo transfer; and watercraft units/teams. It can also control host/ allied nation and indigenous personnel and equipment employed in transportation support of an independent division-size force, two division separate Corps forces, or to provide all transportation services on an area basis, when required.

HHC, TRANSPORTATION TERMINAL BATTALION (TOE 55816L000)

MISSION AND ASSIGNMENT

C-A-6. To provide command and control, planning, and supervision of attached units employed in the operation of a water terminal. The HQ company provides unit administration and logistical support for the battalion staff sections. This organization is assigned to a theater TRANSCOM normally attached to a transportation composite group.

CAPABILITIES

C-A-7. This unit provides:

- Command and control, planning, and supervision of attached units required to load/unload up to four ships simultaneously at an established water terminal or up to two ships simultaneously at a LOTS site.

- The command element for operation of intermediate staging areas of airborne units.

- The command element for operation of inland waterways and support of amphibious operations.
- Food service support for the MCT (region) (TOE 55580LD00).

HHD, MOTOR TRANSPORT BATTALION (TOE 55716L000)

MISSION AND ASSIGNMENT

C-A-8. To provide command, control, and supervision of units engaged in all types of motor transport operations. This organization is assigned to a Corps, attached to a Corps support group or to a TRANSCOM or attached to a transportation composite group.

CAPABILITIES

C-A-9. This unit:

- Provides command, control, and supervision of three to seven transportation companies and attached support units, or a combination thereof.
- Plans and schedules requirements to conform with the overall movement program.
- Translates transportation requirements from higher HQ into specific vehicles or units required.
- Evaluates highway traffic plans affecting road movement, to include terrain, road conditions, and security.
- Supervises the operation of truck terminals, TTPs, and/or a trailer relay system.
- Coordinates HNS.
- Provides religious support to attached units.
- Provides unit maintenance on communications/electronic equipment, except communications security equipment for attached units.

Annex B

Movement Control

Need lead in when this FM is updated.

TRANSPORTATION MOVEMENT CONTROL AGENCY (TOE 55603L000)

MISSION AND ASSIGNMENT

C-B-1. To command and supervise attached or assigned units and teams engaged in movement control and highway regulation. To provide movements management, highway regulation, and coordination as required, for personnel and materiel movements into, within, and out of the TA. This organization is assigned to the TA.

CAPABILITIES

C-B-2. At level 1, on a 24-hour basis, this unit provides command and control of assigned or attached units or teams. When augmented by teams from TOE 55580LXXX, this unit provides:

- Central organization and field offices necessary to perform movement control services in support of a TA.

- Supplemental movement management for personnel and materiel (except bulk POL by pipeline) into, within, or out of the TA.

- Highway regulation within the TA.

TRANSPORTATION MOVEMENT CONTROL CENTER (TOE 55604L000)

MISSION AND ASSIGNMENT

C-B-3. MCC provides centralized movement control and highway regulation in the Corps AO. The Corps G4 exercises staff supervision for movements and oversees the fulfillment of the commander's logistics priorities.

CAPABILITIES

C-B-4. The MCC provides movement control for personnel, mail, and materiel moving into, within, or out of the Corps area. It accomplishes this mission by using attached MCTs and movement regulation teams.

MOVEMENT CONTROL TEAM, REGION (TOE 55580LD00)

MISSION AND ASSIGNMENT

C-B-5. To perform movement control functions for personnel and material (except bulk POL). Teams are normally assigned to a Transportation Movement Control Agency or Transportation MCC. Teams may be attached or assigned to other transportation units or they may be organized into structured units to meet requirements not provided for in standard TOE.

CAPABILITIES

C-B-6. Coordinates the activities of up to ten subordinate MCTs on a two-shift basis. May be used as a movement element in support of tactical force where employment of a transportation MCC is not warranted.

MOVEMENT CONTROL TEAM (TOE 55580LA00)
MISSION AND ASSIGNMENT

C-B-7. Provides technical expertise in the functional areas of transportation, medical services, adjutant general, and supply to coordinate with functional counterparts in the TA area command and COSCOM. The teams are normally assigned to a Transportation Movement Control Agency or Transportation MCC. Teams may be attached or assigned to other transportation units or they may be organized into structured units to meet requirements not provided for in standard TOE.

CAPABILITIES

C-B-8. The team provides liaison with the US Air Force terminal commander on matters associated with expediting the clearance of Army cargo and personnel arriving by US Air Force aircraft and coordinating local movement of retrograde or resupply cargo and personnel as required for deployment movement of Army tactical forces.

MOVEMENT CONTROL TEAM (TOE 55580LB000)
MISSION AND ASSIGNMENT

C-B-9. To perform movement control functions for personnel and material (except bulk POL by pipeline). The teams are normally assigned to a Transportation Movement Control Agency or Transportation MCC. Teams may be attached or assigned to other transportation units or they may be organized into structured units to meet requirements not provided for in standard TOE.

CAPABILITIES

C-B-10. Provides single-shift movement control functions at a two ship LOTS terminal, one or two ship fixed water terminal, or an inland transfer point. Attachment of one or more additional like teams can be structured to provide multiple shift capability.

MOVEMENT CONTROL TEAM (TOE 55580LC00)
MISSION AND ASSIGNMENT

C-B-11. To perform movement control functions for personnel and material (except bulk POL by pipeline). The teams are normally assigned to a Transportation Movement Control Agency or Transportation MCC. Teams may be attached or assigned to other transportation units or they may be organized into structured units to meet requirements not provided for in standard TOE.

CAPABILITIES

C-B-12. Provides single-shift movement control functions in support of GS supply and/or maintenance activities, a four ship fixed water terminal operation, or a rail or motor terminal. Attachment of one or more additional like teams can be structured to provide multiple shift capability.

MOVEMENT CONTROL TEAM, AIR TERMINAL (TOE 55580LF00)

MISSION AND ASSIGNMENT

C-B-13. To coordinate the expeditious clearance of Army cargo and personnel from US Air Force terminals and the arrival of retrograde or resupply cargo and personnel. The teams are normally assigned to a Transportation Movement Control Agency or Transportation MCC. Teams may be attached or assigned to other transportation units or they may be organized into structured units to meet requirements not provided for in standard TOE.

CAPABILITIES AND FUNCTIONS

C-B-14. Performs the following movement control functions on a two-shift basis:

- Expedites the clearance of Army cargo and personnel arriving at a US Air Force terminal.

- Coordinates local movement of retrograde or resupply cargo and personnel.

- Provides technical expertise in the functional areas of transportation, medical services, adjutant general, and supply to coordinate with functional counterparts in the TA area command and/or COSCOM.

- Provides liaison with the US Air Force terminal which requires coordination of movement of Army cargo and personnel in accordance with stated capabilities.

MOVEMENT CONTROL TEAM, HIGHWAY REGULATION POINT (TOE 55580LH00)

MISSION AND ASSIGNMENT

C-B-15. To operate a highway regulation point. To coordinate the movement of authorized traffic and to effect changes in truck or convoy routings. The teams are normally assigned to a Transportation Movement Control Agency or Transportation MCC. Teams may be attached or organized into structured units to meet requirements not provided for in standard TOE.

CAPABILITIES

C-B-16. Observes, follows, and reports progress of vehicles along routes and adjusts movement schedules as necessary on a single-shift basis. Attachment of one or more like teams can be structured to provide multiple shift capability.

Terminal Operations

Need lead in when this FM is updated.

TRANSPORTATION COMPANY (CARGO TRANSFER)

MISSION AND ASSIGNMENT

C-C-1. To discharge, load, and transship cargo at air, rail, or truck terminals; to discharge, load, and transship cargo at water terminals located in fixed ports or in LOTS operations; and supplement cargo/supply handling operations at CSS activities in corps and division areas to alleviate cargo backlogs. At level 1, this unit can operate up to four rail, truck, or air terminals on a 24-hour per day basis. The size of the terminal and/or scope of the operation may mean that more than one platoon is required to operate a given terminal.

CAPABILITIES

C-C-2. The daily capability of this unit is as follows:

- In rail or truck terminal operations tranship; 820 STONs of breakbulk cargo or 200 containers per terminal. For a four terminal, a total of 3,280 STONs of breakbulk or 800 containers, or a combination thereof.

- In air terminal operations transship; 550 STONs of non-containerized cargo or 160, 20-foot container equivalents per terminal. For a four terminal, a total of 2,200 STONs of non-containerized cargo or 640, 20-foot container equivalents, or a combination thereof.

- In a fixed port accomplish one, but not all of the following:

  - Given a container ship and pier side cranes, discharge or load 500 containers per day, or a combination thereof.

  - When augmented by the port operations cargo detachment, discharge or load 2,500 STONs of breakbulk cargo. In simultaneous operations, move 1,250 STONs in each direction.

  - With a RO/RO ship, discharge up to 1,000 vehicles or load up to 750 vehicles.

- In a LOTS operation, augmented by the port operations cargo detachment; accomplish one, but not all of the following:

  - Discharge or load 300 containers. In simultaneous operations move 150 containers in each direction.

  - Discharge or load 1,500 STONs of breakbulk cargo. In simultaneous operations move 750 STONs in each direction.

- At inland terminals, can perpetuate cargo documentation and redocument diverted or reconsigned cargo.

- During container operations, can stuff and unstuff containers. However, this capability degrades other capabilities.

TRANSPORTATION CARGO TRANSFER COMPANY, ONE TERMINAL (TOE 55817L100) AND TRANSPORTATION CARGO TRANSFER COMPANY, THREE TERMINALS (TOE 55817L200)

MISSION AND ASSIGNMENT

C-C-3. To transship cargo at air, rail, and motor terminals. This unit is normally assigned to a TA area command or to a COSCOM. Normally attached to a motor transport, terminal, or aviation battalion, as required.

CAPABILITIES

C-C-4. At level 1, the unit has the following capabilities:

- Under 55817L100, is capable of operating a single terminal on a 24-hour basis. It can transship 1,000 STONs of breakbulk or 150 containers daily.

- Under 55817L200, is capable of operating up to three separate terminals on a 24-hour basis. Each terminal can transship 1,000 STONs of breakbulk cargo or 150 containers per day for a unit total of 3,000 STONs of breakbulk cargo or 450 containers daily, or a combination thereof.

FUNCTIONS

C-C-5. The functions of this unit include:

- Redocuments transshipped cargo or containers, as required.

- Has a capability for stuffing and unstuffing containers.

TRANSPORTATION TERMINAL SERVICE COMPANY, BREAKBULK (TOE 55818L000)

MISSION AND ASSIGNMENT

C-C-6. To discharge, backload, and transship breakbulk cargo at water terminals located at beaches or fixed points. This unit is normally assigned to a TRANSCOM or to a COSCOM when employed to support independent Corps operations. Normally attached to a Transportation Terminal Battalion.

CAPABILITIES

C-C-7. On a two-shift basis with 75 percent operational availability of all mission equipment, this unit is capable of the following:

- In a LOTS operation, discharging 1,600 STONs of breakbulk cargo or backloading at the same rate or simultaneously discharging 800 STONs of breakbulk cargo and backloading 800 STONs of breakbulk cargo.

- In a fixed port operation, discharging 2,500 STONs of breakbulk cargo or backloading at the same rate or simultaneously discharging 1,250 STONs of breakbulk cargo and backloading 1,250 STONs.

- Sorting breakbulk cargo by destination and loading breakbulk cargo from the marshaling yards on land transportation.

- Providing limited in-transit storage.

TRANSPORTATION TERMINAL SERVICE COMPANY, CONTAINER/BREAKBULK (TOE 55827L000)

MISSION AND ASSIGNMENT

C-C-8. To discharge, backload, and transship breakbulk and containerized cargo at water terminals located at fixed ports or in LOTS operations. This unit is assigned to a TRANSCOM or to a COSCOM when employed to support independent Corps operations. Normally attached to a Transportation Terminal Battalion.

CAPABILITIES

C-C-9. At level 1, on a two-shift basis with 75 percent operational availability of all mission equipment, this unit is capable of the following:

- In a LOTS operation:

  - When supported by a heavy crane platoon discharging 200 containers or backloading at the same rate or simultaneously discharging 100 containers and backloading 100 containers.

  - Discharging 1,600 STONs of breakbulk cargo or backloading at the same rate simultaneously discharging 800 STONs of breakbulk cargo and backloading 800 STONs.

  - Sorting breakbulk and containers by designation, loading breakbulk cargo and containers from the marshaling yards on land transportation, and performing limited stuffing and unstuffing of containers.

  - Receiving and processing containers for retrograde.

- In a fixed port operation:

  - When supported by a heavy crane platoon discharging 400 containers or backloading at the same rate or simultaneously discharging 200 containers and backloading 200 containers.

  - Discharging 2,500 STONs of breakbulk cargo or backloading at the same rate or simultaneously discharging 1,250 STONs of breakbulk cargo and backloading 1,250 STONs.

  - Sorting breakbulk and containers by destination, loading breakbulk cargo and containers from the marshaling yards on land transportation, and performing limited stuffing and unstuffing of containers.

  - Receiving and processing containers for retrograde.

  - Providing limited in-transit storage.

TRANSPORTATION MEDIUM WATERCRAFT COMPANY (TOE 55828L0)

MISSION AND ASSIGNMENT

C-C-10. To provide and operate landing craft for the movement of personnel and cargo in Army water terminal operations and Army waterborne tactical operations and to augment, when required, naval craft in joint amphibious operations. This unit is assigned to a transportation command or COSCOM. Normally attached to a Transportation Terminal Battalion or a Transportation Terminal Group.

CAPABILITIES

C-C-11. At level 1, based on a 75 percent availability of landing craft and operating on a 24-hour basis, this unit is capable of the following:

- Transporting an average of 1,000 STONs of non-containerized cargo based on an average of 42 STONs per landing craft, each making two trips daily.

- Transporting 240, 20-foot containers per day based on one container per landing craft, each making 20 trips daily.

- Transporting 2,400 combat equipped troops, each making one trip per day.

TRANSPORTATION HEAVY WATERCRAFT COMPANY (TOE 55829L000)
MISSION AND ASSIGNMENT

C-C-12. To provide and operate landing craft for the transportation of personnel, containers, and out-sized cargo in offshore discharge operations and lighterage service. This organization is assigned to a TRANSCOM normally attached to a Transportation Terminal Battalion or a transportation composite group. May be attached in support of a joint amphibious operation or may operate separately under an appropriate commander.

CAPABILITIES

C-C-13. At level 1, based on a 75 percent availability of landing craft operating on a 24-hour basis, this unit is capable of the following:

- Transporting 1,600 STONs of non-containerized cargo, each making one trip daily.

- Transporting 288 containers, each making 7.2 trips daily.

- Transporting 3,200 combat-equipped personnel, each making one trip daily.

LIGHTER AMPHIBIOUS, LARC LX DETACHMENT (TOE 55530LH00)
MISSION AND ASSIGNMENT

C-C-14. To provide command and control of amphibious lighterage service primarily for items of heavy, outsized, or bulky equipment. Is assigned to a TRANSCOM and attached to a TRANSPORTATION TERMINAL BATTALION.

CAPABILITIES

C-C-15. This team, with a 75 percent availability and operating on a 24-hour basis, can transport 450 STONs of heavy, outsized or bulky non-containerized cargo in 5 trips (30 STONs per lighter, per trip). It can also transport 72, 20-foot containers or 2,625 combat-equipped troops in 12 trips. Performs unit maintenance on all organic equipment, except communications security equipment and DS/GS maintenance on amphibious equipment.

LOGISTICAL SUPPORT VESSEL DETACHMENT (TOE 55530LJ00)
MISSION AND ASSIGNMENT

C-C-16. To provide transportation for vehicles and/or general cargo to remote, underdeveloped areas along coastlines and inland waterways; to support unit deployments, relocations, and port to port operations; and to assist in discharging and backloading ships in a RO/RO or LOTS operation. This unit is assigned to a TRANSCOM and attached to a Transportation Terminal Battalion.

CAPABILITIES

C-C-17. This team is capable of self-sustainment for a period of 30 to 45 days with accommodations for a 29-member crew.

FUNCTIONS

C-C-18. This team is responsible for the following:

- Transports 2,016 STONs of cargo, consisting of vehicles, containers, and/or general cargo.
- Loads, transports (in integral tanks), and offloads 11,000 barrels of bulk liquid cargo.
- Transports three liquid products simultaneously (jet fuel, MOGAS, and diesel).
- Transfers products to or from another vessel or fixed facility.
- Receives and discharges cargo through a bow ramp or stern ramp.
- Beaches with a 1:30 offshore gradient with a maximum of 900 STONs of cargo.
- Performs unit maintenance on all organic equipment, except communications security equipment and DS maintenance on vessel equipment.
- Provides unit-level health services and food service support.
- Is capable of self-delivery to a theater of operations and meets the requirements to transit the Panama and Suez Canals.

TRANSPORTATION FLOATING CRAFT GS MAINTENANCE COMPANY (TOE 55613L000)

MISSION AND ASSIGNMENT

C-C-19. Provides intermediate GS maintenance for US Army landing craft, amphibians and intermediate DS, and intermediate GS maintenance for harbor craft. This unit is assigned to a TRANSCOM or composite group. May be attached to a Transportation Terminal Battalion or may operate independently under the supervision of an appropriate commander.

CAPABILITIES

C-C-20. This unit is capable of providing annual man-hours of productive maintenance (approximate) at levels 1, 2, and 3 as shown in the following table:

	Level 1	Level 2	Level 3
Diving	21,700	21,700	18,600
Hull Repair	86,800	74,400	65,100
Instrument Repair	3,100	3,100	3,100
Machining	24,800	21,700	18,600
Marine Electrical Repair	18,600	18,600	12,400
Marine Engine Repair	55,800	49,600	43,400
Power General Equipment Repair	12,400	9,300	6,200
Plumbing and Pipe-fitting	9,300	9,300	9,300
Radar Repair	9,300	6,200	6,200
Radio Repair	12,400	12,400	9,300
Refrigeration	15,500	15,500	15,500
Rigging Repair	12,400	9,300	9,300
Sheet Metal Working	12,400	9,300	9,300
Welder (Blacksmithing)	12,400	9,300	9,300

NOTE: Availability criteria based on category 3 (mobile) units, allowing 3,100 annual productive man-hours per authorized repairman/technician in accordance with AR 570-2.

TRANSPORTATION TERMINAL SERVICE AUGMENTATION TEAMS

TOE 55560LA00, Cargo Documentation Team (Augmentation)
TOE 55560LB00, Freight Consolidation and Distribution Team (Augmentation)
TOE 55560LC00, Transportation Contract Supervision Team (Augmentation)
TOE 55560LD00, Automated Cargo Documentation Team (Augmentation)
TOE 55560LE00, Heavy Crane Platoon (Augmentation)
TOE 55560LF00, Port Operations Cargo Detachment

MISSION AND ASSIGNMENT

C-C-21. To relocate heavy maneuver forces on the battlefield. These teams may be assigned to a TRANSCOM or COSCOM; attached to a HHC, Transportation Terminal Battalion, HHD, Transportation Motor Transport Battalion, or HHD, Corps Support Battalion.

CAPABILITIES

C-C-22. Individual characteristics are described below:

Cargo Documentation Team

C-C-23. Provides documentation required in the loading and unloading of up to 500 STONs of general cargo or 480 containers daily in an air, rail, truck, or water terminal.

Freight Consolidation and Distribution Team

C-C-24. Processes 100 less-than-carload shipments daily in a consolidation and distribution point; barge site; air, rail, truck, or water terminal; and stuffs or unstuffs 25, 20-foot containers daily.

Transportation Contract Supervision Team

C-C-25. This team provides:

- Administration of contracts made to accomplish the loading, unloading, terminal clearance, and transportation of cargo.

- Loading or unloading of cargo from ships or barges.

- Clearance of unloaded cargo from the terminal by contract.

- Movement of cargo from terminals, depots, or local procurement sources by inland waterways and highways transport contracts.

Automated Cargo Documentation Team

C-C-26. This team provides:

- Documentation of breakbulk, vehicles, or container cargo being loaded or unloaded for up to four ships in a fixed port operation or two ships in a LOTS operation.

- A light wheeled vehicle mechanic to the attached unit providing maintenance support.

- A cook to the attached unit providing food service support.

Heavy Crane Platoon

C-C-27. This platoon provides:

- Personnel and equipment to handle 400 containers in a fixed port operation.

- Personnel and equipment to handle 200 containers in a LOTS operation.

- Unit maintenance on organic equipment, except communications-electronic equipment, and performs DS/GS maintenance on container handling equipment.

- A cook to the attached unit providing food service support.

Port Operations Cargo Detachment

C-C-28. This detachment provides the cargo transfer company with the capability to accomplish one of the following:

- LOTS operations:

  - Discharge or load 1,500 STONs of breakbulk cargo. In simultaneous operations move 750 STONs in each direction.

  - Discharge or load 300 containers. In simultaneous operations move 150 containers.

- In fixed operations, accomplish one of the following:

  - Given a crane ship and pier side cranes, discharge or load 500 containers per day, or combination thereof.

  - Discharge or load 2,500 STONs of breakbulk cargo. In simultaneous operations, move 1,250 STONs in each direction.

- Provides two cooks to augment food service capability of the supported unit.

Annex D

Highway

Need lead in when this FM is updated.

TRAILER TRANSFER POINT (TOE 55540LEOD)
MISSION AND ASSIGNMENT

C-D-1. To operate a TTP in conjunction with line-haul operations. This team is assigned to a transportation motor transport battalion or group.

CAPABILITIES

C-D-2. Operates on a single shift basis, in conjunction with a line-haul operation, with a maximum capacity of 125 semitrailer units in and out of the trailer transfer point.

FUNCTIONS

C-D-3. This team is responsible for the following:

- The operation includes receiving, segregating, assembling, and dispatching loaded or empty semitrailers for convoys.
- Maintaining POL dispensing facilities to refuel operating equipment.
- Servicing, inspecting, and if required, making emergency repairs to incoming vehicles.
- Preparing and maintaining required operational records and reports.

TRANSPORTATION MOTOR TRANSPORT COMPANY, MAIN SUPPORT BATTALION, AIRBORNE DIVISION (TOE 55158L000)
MISSION AND ASSIGNMENT

C-D-4. To provide truck transportation for distribution of Class I, II, III (packaged), IV, VII and IX supplies within the division area, transport troops in support of division operations, and provide supplemental transportation to include emergency unit distribution of Class V supplies and water. This unit is organic to the Main Support Battalion, Airborne Division.

CAPABILITIES

C-D-5. Provides drivers and control personnel for one shift operation of all unit task vehicles. For planning purposes, based upon 75 percent of the task vehicles available, this unit has the capability to do the following:

- Provide the following task vehicles on a daily basis: Truck, cargo, 5 tons (30 trucks); tractor, 5 tons, with cargo.

- Make a one-time breakbulk cargo lift of 30 trucks, 2-1/2 tons X 2.5 ton per vehicle load (75 STONs); seven 5-ton trucks, tractors, with semitrailers X 15 tons per vehicle.

- Make a one-time troop lift of seven 5-ton trucks, tractors, with semitrailers X 35 troops per vehicle.

TRANSPORTATION MOTOR TRANSPORT COMPANY, MAIN SUPPORT BATTALION, AIR ASSAULT DIVISION (TOE 55168L000)

MISSION AND ASSIGNMENT

C-D-6. To provide truck transportation for unit distribution of Class II, IV, VII, and IX supplies. To transport troops in support of division operations. To transport the division reserve supplies for which the supply and transport battalion is responsible. To furnish vehicles to assist division elements with a requirement for supplemental transportation to include emergency unit distribution of water and Class V supplies. This unit is organic to the MSB, Air Assault Division.

CAPABILITIES

C-D-7. Provides sufficient drivers and control personnel for one shift operation of all unit task vehicles.

FUNCTIONS

C-D-8. For planning purposes, based upon 75 percent of the task vehicles available, this unit has the capability to do the following:

- Provide the following task vehicles daily: Truck, cargo, 5 tons, (30 trucks), truck, tractor, 5 tons, with cargo semitrailer.

- Make a one-time breakbulk cargo lift with 30 trucks, 5 tons X 5 tons per vehicle load. Seven 5-ton trucks, tractors, with semitrailers X 15 tons per vehicle load.

- Make a one-time troop lift with 30 trucks, 5 tons X 20 troops per vehicle. Seven 5-ton trucks, tractors, with semitrailers X 35 troops per vehicle.

TRANSPORTATION MOTOR TRANSPORT COMPANY, LIGHT INFANTRY DIVISION (TOE 55178L000)

MISSION AND ASSIGNMENT

C-D-9. Provide truck transportation for unit distribution of Class II, IV, VII, and IX supplies, transport troops in support of division operations, and transport the division reserve supplies for which the supply and transport battalion is responsible. It also provides supplemental transportation for division elements to include emergency unit distribution of Class V and water. This unit is organic to the MSB, Light Infantry Division.

CAPABILITIES

C-D-10. With 75 percent task vehicle availability, this unit provides sufficient drivers and control personnel for a 24-hour operation of the unit's task vehicles.

FUNCTIONS

C-D-11. The following task vehicles are dispatched daily:

- Truck, cargo, 5 tons (24 trucks), truck, tractor, 5 tons, with semitrailer, 22-1/2 tons.

- The one-time lift of non-containerized cargo is accomplished by 24 trucks, cargo, 5 tons X 5 tons per vehicle load.

TRANSPORTATION MOTOR TRANSPORT COMPANY, MAIN SUPPORT BATTALION, HEAVY DIVISION (TOE 55188L000)

MISSION AND ASSIGNMENT

C-D-12. To provide truck transportation for the distribution of supplies and the movement of heavy and/or outsized vehicles and cargo. It also furnishes vehicles to assist division elements requiring supplemental transportation to include emergency unit distribution of Class V. This unit is organic to a MSB, Heavy Division.

CAPABILITIES

C-D-13. With 75 percent task vehicle availability, this unit provides sufficient drivers and control personnel for a 24-hour operation of the unit's task vehicles.

FUNCTIONS

C-D-14. The following task vehicles are dispatched daily:

- Truck, cargo, 5 tons, (27 trucks), truck, tractor, 5 tons, with semitrailer, 22-1/2 tons, 24 trucks, tractor, heavy equipment transport with semitrailer, low-bed.

- A one-time lift of non-containerized using 27 trucks, cargo, 5 tons X 5 tons per vehicle load.

- Twenty-four trucks, tractor with semitrailer, 22-1/2 tons X 15 tons per semi-trailer load.

- Eighteen heavy equipment transports X 40 tons per semitrailer load.

- Eighteen heavy equipment transports X 18 tanks or 1 tank or tank equivalent tank per semitrailer equivalent.

TRANSPORTATION LIGHT TRUCK COMPANY (TOE 55718L200/55718L100)
MISSION AND ASSIGNMENT

C-D-15. To provide truck transportation for the movement of general cargo and personnel. This unit is normally assigned to the TRANSCOM or COSCOM. However, it is normally attached to a transportation motor transport battalion.

CAPABILITIES

C-D-16. With a 75 percent vehicle availability, this unit, operating on a two shift basis, making four round trips per day (two per operating shift) in local-hauls and two round trips per day (one per the following):

- Local-hauls. 400 STONs of cargo (2-1/2 tons per truck) on road or 3,600 passengers (20 passengers per truck).
- Line-hauls. 200 STONs of cargo (2-1/2 tons per truck) on road or 1,620 passengers (18 passengers per truck).

TRANSPORTATION LIGHT MEDIUM TRUCK COMPANY (TOE 55719L100)
MISSION AND ASSIGNMENT

C-D-17. To provide transportation for the movement of non-containerized cargo and personnel by motor transport. This unit is normally assigned to a COSCOM and attached to a HHD, Corps Support Battalion.

CAPABILITIES

C-D-18. At level 1, with a 75 percent task vehicle availability, these units are capable of transporting the following:

- This unit, operating on a one-shift basis, making two round trips per day in local-hauls or one round trip per day in line/long hauls is shown as follows:

CARGO	LOCAL-HAULS	LINE/LONG HAUL
Non-containerized (5 STONs per truck)	375 STONs	187.5 STONs
Personnel	20 per truck	16 per truck
Semitrailer (15 STONs per transporter)	225 STONs	112.5 STONs

- Under emergency conditions, 50 seated passengers may be transported per semitrailer.

TRANSPORTATION/CARGO MEDIUM TRUCK COMPANY (TOE 55727L100) AND PETROLEUM MEDIUM TRUCK COPMPANY (TOE 55727L200)

MISSION AND ASSIGNMENT

C-D-19. To provide transportation for the movement of containerized, non-containerized, palletized, dry and/or refrigerated containerized cargo, and bulk water products, when organized under TOE 55727L100 and bulk petroleum products when organized under TOE 55727L200. This unit is assigned to a TRANSCOM, normally attached to a HHD, Transportation Motor Transport Battalion.

CAPABILITIES

C-D-20. At level 1, with a 75 percent task vehicle availability, these units, operating on a two-shift basis, making four round-trips per day (two per operating shift) in local-hauls or two round-trips (one per operating shift) in line-hauls, are capable of transporting the following.

- TOE 55727L100:

CARGO	LOCAL-HAULS	LINE/LONG HAUL
Containers (Dry/Refrigerated) (Maximum 24 STONs per transporter	40 ft - 180 20 ft - 360	90
Non-containerized (Palletized/Packaged) (Maximum 22 STONs per transporter)	3,960 STONs	1,980 STONs
Water (4,750 gallons per transporter)	855,000 gallons	427,500 gallons

PERSONNEL: Under emergency conditions, 50 seated passengers may be transported per semitrailer.

- TOE 55727L200:

CARGO	LOCAL-HAULS	LINE/LONG HAUL
BTOE	900,000 gallons	450,000 gallons
OTOE	1,350,000 gallons	675,000 gallons

TRANSPORTATION MEDIUM TRUCK COMPANY, 20 FOOT CONTAINER/CARGO (TOE 55728L100)

MISSION AND ASSIGNMENT

C-D-21. To provide transportation for the movement of and/or refrigerated containerized cargo. This unit is assigned to a COSCOM or TA Area Command.

CAPABILITIES

C-D-22. At level 1, with a 75 percent task vehicle availability, this unit operating on a two-shift basis, making four round trips per day in local hauls. In line hauls it is capable of two round trips per day.

TRANSPORTATION MEDIUM TRUCK COMPANY, 5,000 GALLON TANKER (TOE 55728L200)

MISSION AND ASSIGNMENT

C-D-23. To provide transportation for the movement of petroleum. This unit is assigned to a COSCOM or TA Area Command.

CAPABILITIES

C-D-24. At level 1, with a 75 percent task vehicle availability, this unit provides retail distribution of petroleum products, vehicle refueling, and open refueling of aircraft, if required.

TRANSPORTATION MEDIUM TRUCK COMPANY, PLS (TOE 55728L300)

MISSION AND ASSIGNMENT

C-D-25. To provide transportation for the movement of cargo. This unit is assigned to a COSCOM or TA Area Command.

CAPABILITIES

C-D-26. At level 1, with a 75 percent task vehicle availability, this unit, operating on a two-shift basis, making four round trips per day in local hauls (3,170 STONs). In line hauls, it is capable of two round trips per day (2,016 STONs).

TRANSPORTATION HEAVY TRUCK COMPANY (TOE 55729L000)

MISSION AND ASSIGNMENT

C-D-27. To provide truck transportation for the movement of tanks and/or other outsized vehicles and breakbulk cargo. This unit is normally assigned to a Corps or TA. It may be attached to a Corps Support Battalion or to a Transport Battalion.

CAPABILITIES

C-D-28. At level 1, with a 90 percent task vehicle availability, this unit, operating on a two shift basis, making four round trips per day (two per operating shift). For local hauls with 21 transporter combinations available can move 84 tanks or 3,340 STONs of breakbulk cargo.

COMBAT HEAVY EQUIPMENT TRANSPORT COMPANY (TOE 55739L100/55739L200)

MISSION AND ASSIGNMENT

C-D-29. To relocate heavy maneuver forces on the battlefield. This unit for operational relocation missions, is assigned to a TRANSCOM and attached to a Transportation Motor Transport Battalion. For tactical relocation missions, it is assigned to the Corps and attached to a Transportation Motor Transport Battalion.

CAPABILITIES

C-D-30. At level 1, with a 90 percent task vehicle availability, this unit provides:

- A one-time lift of 86 tracked combat vehicles (one tracked vehicle per heavy equipment transport). Four of these units, operating in concert, can relocate a brigade size heavy maneuver force (with division support slice) provided the special conditions are noted in the following paragraph.

- The capabilities stated above are minimums; double loading of tracked vehicles on heavy equipment transport systems will increase the capability of either variant to the extent that tracked vehicles are doubled loaded. A one-time lift relocation of a heavy maneuver force (with division slice) required double loading of tracked vehicles as much as possible.

Annex E

Rail Operations

Need lead in when this FM is updated.

HHC TRANSPORTATION RAILWAY BATTALION (TOE 55916L00)

MISSION AND ASSIGNMENT

C-E-1. To exercise command, control, and supervision over assigned and attached units and to operate and maintain railway facilities in a theater of operations. This unit, assigned to a TRANSCOM, may be further attached to a Headquarters, Headquarters Company transportation composite group.

CAPABILITIES

C-E-2. At level 1, this unit can do the following:

- Provides command, staff planning, unit administration, control, and supervision of operations of all assigned and attached units.

- Operates and maintains a railway division of approximately 90 to 150 miles (145 to 240 kilometers).

- Dispatches all trains, supervises on-line operations, and operates railway stations and signal towers for which it has responsibility.

- Maintains a consolidated property book for assigned units.

TRANSPORTATION RAILWAY ENGINEERING COMPANY (TOE 55918L00)

MISSION AND ASSIGNMENT

C-E-3. To maintain and repair railway track, bridges, buildings, and structures within a railway division. This unit is assigned to a TRANSCOM and to a HHC, Transportation Railway Battalion.

CAPABILITIES

C-E-4. At level 1, this unit provides:

- Maintenance and repair of track, bridges, buildings, and structures of a railway division of approximately 90 to 150 miles (145 to 240 kilometers).

- Vehicular maintenance for HHC, Transportation Railway Battalion and Transportation Train Operating Company.

TRANSPORTATION TRAIN OPERATING COMPANY (TOE 55927L000) (30 train crews) or (TOE 755927L200) (50 train crews)

MISSION AND ASSIGNMENT

C-E-5. To operate railway locomotives and trains. This unit is normally attached to a transportation railway battalion or may operate separately under the supervision of appropriate transportation element.

CAPABILITIES

C-E-6. At level 1, on a 24-hour basis, this unit:

- Operates trains and locomotives in both yard and road service and performs incidental switching service for a railway division 90 to 150 miles (145 to 241 kilometers) long.

- Performs switching and train build up in a large terminal including port clearance of up to a 20 mile (32 kilometers) radius from a large port.

- Provides up to 50 train crews daily for road or terminal operations including switching, classifying, and making up trains for the road.

TRANSPORTATION RAILWAY EQUIPMENT MAINTENANCE COMPANY (TOE 55919L000)

MISSION AND ASSIGNMENT

C-E-7. To inspect, service, and make running repairs to diesel-electric locomotives and rolling stock. This unit is normally attached to a transportation railway battalion. It may operate separately under supervision of appropriate transportation element.

CAPABILITIES

C-E-8. At level 1, this unit:

- Services 40 diesel-electric locomotives and performs running inspections on 200 railway cars daily.

- Makes running repairs on 40 diesel-electric locomotives and 800 railway cars annually.

- Performs light repairs to tools and limited repairs to special mechanical equipment within the battalion.

- Provides wreck train support to the battalion.

Annex F

Host Nation Support Team

Need lead in when this FM is updated.

TRANSPORTATION HOST NATION SUPPORT TEAM (TOE 55510LA00)

MISSION AND ASSIGNMENT

C-F-1. To serve as a liaison and interface between US unique transportation systems and HN terminal transfer units. Assigned to a COSCOM when employed in a Corps area or to a TRANSCOM when employed at EAC and attached to a HN transportation battalion.

CAPABILITIES

C-F-2. Provides operational mission coordination functions (taskings) to HN transportation battalion consisting of various transportation truck units and two terminal transfer companies.

FUNCTIONS

C-F-3. This team is responsible for the following:

- Consolidates and forwards transportation management reports from HN units.
- Coordinates mission taskings between US MCC and HN terminal transfer units.
- This unit is not adaptable to a type B organization.
- Individuals of this organization can assist in the coordinated defense of the unit's area or installation.

Glossary

AAFES	Army and Air Force Exchange Service
ABCCS	Army Global Command Control System
ABCS	Army Battle Command System
ACOM	Atlantic Command
ACR	armored cavalry regiment
A/DACG	arrival/departure airfield control group
ADANS	Airlift Deployment Analysis System
ADP	automatic data processing
AFATDS	Advanced Field Artillery Tactical Data System
AFFOR	Air Force forces
AFSCC	Air Force Service Component Commander
AIT	Automatic Identification Technology
AMC	Air Mobility Command
AMOPES	Army Mobilization and Operations Planning and Execution System
AO	area of operations
AOR	area of responsibility
APOD	aerial port of debarkation
APOE	aerial port of embarkation
AR	Army regulation
ARFOR	Army forces
ASAS	All Source Analysis System
ASCC	Army Service Component Commander
ASPUR	Automated System for Processing Unit Requirements
ATCCS	Army Tactical Command and Control System
ATMCT	Air Terminal Movement Control Team
ATP	Ammunition Transfer Point
AUEL	Automated Unit Equipment List
AWIS	Army WWMCCS Information System
B2C2	Brigade and Below Command and Control System
BSA	brigade support area

C2	command and control
CAA	command arrangement agreement
CAP	crisis action planning
CAPS II	Consolidated Aerial Port System II
CD-ROM	compact disk-read only memory
CENTCOM	Central Command
CIA	Central Intelligence Agency
CINC	Commander in Chief
CJCS	Chairman, Joint Chiefs of Staff
CJTF	Commanders Joint Task Force
CLT	cellular logistics team
CMAA	Cooperative Military Airlift Agreement
CMOC	Civil Military Operations Center
COCOM	combatant command
COMPASS	Computerized Movement Planning and Status System
CONPLAN	concept plan
CONUS	continental United States
CONUSA	the numbered armies in the continental United States
CORE	contingency response program
COSCOM	corps support command
CRAF	Civil Reserve Air Fleet
CSG	Corps Support Group
CSS	combat service support
CSSCS	Combat Service Support Control System
CTO	Corps Transportation Officer
DA	Department of the Army
DAAS	Defense Automatic Addressing System
DAMMS-R	Department of the Army Movement Management System-Redesign
DASPS-E	Department of the Army Standard Port System-Enhanced
DCSLOG	Deputy Chief of Staff for Logistics
DCSLOG TRANS	Deputy Chief of Staff for Logistics for Transportation
DCSOPS	Deputy Chief of Staff for Operations and Plans
DDN	defense data network
Dept	Department

DFRIF	Defense Freight Railway Interchange Fleet
DFSC	Defense Fuel Supply Center
DIRMOBFOR	Director of Mobility Forces
DISCOM	division support command
DLA	Defense Logistics Agency
DMA	Defense Mapping Agency
DMC	defense movement coordinator
DMMC	division materiel management center
DOD	Department of Defense
DOL	Directorate of Logistics
DOMS	Directorate of Military Support
DOT	Department of Transportation
DPG	defense planning guidance
DS	direct support
DSA	division support area
DSB	Deployment Support Brigade
DSU	direct support unit
DTAV	Department of Defense Total Asset Visibility
DTO	Division Transportation Officer
DTS	Defense Transportation System
DTTS	Defense Transportation Tracking System
EAC	echelons above corps
EPW	enemy prisoner of war
EUCOM	European Command
FAA	Federal Aviation Administration
FAADC2	Forward Area Air Defense Command and Control System
FEMA	Federal Emergency Management Agency
FHWA	Federal Highway Administration
FM	field manual
FORSCOM	United States Army Forces Command
FRA	Federal Railroad Administration
FSB	Forward Support Battalion
ft	feet/foot

G1	Assistant Chief of Staff, G1 (Personnel)
G3	Assistant Chief of Staff, G3 (Operations and Plans)
G4	Assistant Chief of Staff, G4 (Logistics)
GCCS	Global Command and Control System
GDSS	Global Decision Support System
GRREG	graves registration
GS	general support
GSA	General Services Administration
GSU	general support unit
GTN	Global Transportation Network
HETS	Heavy Equipment Transporter System
HHC	headquarters and headquarters company
HHD	headquarters and headquarters detachment
HN	host nation
HNS	host nation support
HQ	headquarters
HQDA	Headquarters, Department of the Army
IBS	Integrated Booking System
IC3	Integrated Command and Control, and Communications System
ICC	Interstate Commerce Commission
INMARSAT	International Maritime Satellite
IRP	inventory reduction plan
ISB	intermediate staging base
ISO	organization of international standards
ISR	installation situation reports
ITO	installation transportation officer
ITV	in-transit visibility
J4	Logistics Directorate
JCS	Joint Chiefs of Staff
JFC	joint force commander
JLOTS	joint logistics-over-the-shore
JMC	Joint Movement Center
JMPA	Joint Military Postal Activities
JOPES	Joint Operation Planning and Execution System

JPD	Joint Planning Document
JPEC	Joint Planning and Execution Community
JPO	Joint Petroleum Office
JSCP	Joint Strategic Capabilities Plan
JTB	Joint Transportation Board
JTBS	Joint Transportation Board Secretariat
JTF	joint task force
LASH	lighter aboard ship
LOC	lines of communication
LOGMARS	Logistic Application of Automated Marking and Reading System
LO/LO	lift-on/lift-off
LOTS	logistics over the shore operations
LSA	Logistics Sustainability Analysis
LSE	Logistics Support Element
MARAD	Maritime Administration
MBBL	thousands of barrels
MCC	movement control center
MCO	Movement Control Officer
MCT	Movement Control Team
METS	Mechanized Export Traffic System
MHE	materiels handling equipment
MILSTRIP	Military Standard Requisitioning and Issue Procedures
MILVAN	military-owned demountable container
MOBCON	Mobilization Movement Control
MOGAS	motor gasoline
MOU	Memorandum of Understanding
MP	military police
MPSA	Military Postal Service Agency
MRT	Movement Regulations Team
MSB	Main Support Battalion
MSC	Military Sealift Command
MSL	Military Shipping Label
MSR	main supply route
MST	Mission Support Team

MTMC	Military Traffic Management Command
MTON	measurement ton
NATO	North Atlantic Treaty Organization
NAVFOR	Navy forces
NCA	National Command Authority
NCOIC	Noncommissioned officer in charge
NEO	noncombatant evacuation order
NSC	National Security Council
OCONUS	outside continental United States
OET	Office of Emergency Transportation
OFDA	Office of the US Foreign Disaster Assistance
OIC	officer in charge
OOTW	operations other than war
OPCON	operational control
OPLAN	operation plan
OPORD	operation order
OPSEC	operations security
OSD	Office of the Secretary of Defense
PACOM	Pacific Command
PLS	Palletized Load System
POD	port of debarkation
POE	port of embarkation
POL	petroleum, oil, and lubricants
POM	program objective memorandum
PRAMS	Passenger Reservation and Manifesting System
PSA	port support activity
PSC	port security company
Publication	publication
RC	Reserve Components
RDD	required delivery date
RF	radio frequency
RO/RO	roll on/roll off
ROS	reduced operational status
Rqmts	requirements
RRF	Ready Reserve Force

S4	Supply Officer (U.S. Army)
SEABEE	sea barge
SECDEF	Secretary of Defense
SMCC	state movement control center
SOCOM	Special Operations Command
SOFOR	Special Operations forces
SOUTHCOM	Southern Command
SPACECOM	Space Command
SPOD	sea port of debarkation
SPOE	sea port of embarkation
STACCS	Standard Theater Army Command and Control System
STAMIS	Standard Army Management Information System
STARC	State Area Command
STON	short ton
STRATCOM	Strategic Command
TA	theater Army
TAA	Tactical Assembly Area
TACC	tanker airlift control center
TALCE	tanker airlift control element
TALO	Tactical Air Liaison Officer
TAMCA	Theater Army Movements Control Agency
TAV	Total Asset Visibility
TB	technical bulletin
TC-ACCIS	Transportation Coordinators-Automated Command and Control Information System
TC-AIMS	Transportation Coordinators-Automated Information for Movements System
TCC	Transportation Component Command
TDA	tables of distribution and allowances
TEU	twenty-foot equivalent units
TMO	Traffic Management Office
TMT	transportation motor transport
TOE	table(s) of organization and equipment
TPFDD	Time-Phased Force Deployment Data
TPFDL	Time-Phased Force Deployment List

TRANSCOM	Transportation Command
TSM	terminal support module
TTB	Transportation Terminal Battalion or Brigade
TTP	trailer transfer point
TUCHA	type unit characteristics data
TVA	Tennessee Valley Authority
UMC	unit movement coordinator
UMD	unit movement data
UMT	Unit Movement Team
UN	United Nations
US	United States (of America)
USA	United States Army
USACOM	United States Atlantic Command
USAF	United States Air Force
USAR	United States Army Reserve
USCG	United States Coast Guard
USCINCTRANS	Commander in Chief, Transportation Comand
USMC	United States Marine Corps
USN	United States Navy
USPS	United States Postal Service
USTRANSCOM	United States Transportation Command
WASP	War Air Service Program
WDIP	Warfighter Deployment Interface Program
WPS	Worldwide Ports System
WWMCCS	Worldwide Military Command and Control System

Bibliography

SOURCES USED

These are the sources quoted or paraphrased in this publication.

AR 5-9. *Intraservice Support Installation Area Coordination.* 1 March 1984.

AR 55-355. *Defense Traffic Management Regulation.* 31 July 1986.

AR 570-2. *Manpower Requirements Criteria.* 15 May 1992.

FM 10-1. *Quartermaster Principles.* 11 August 1994.

FM 10-67. *Petroleum Supply in Theaters of Operations.* 16 February 1983.

FM 54-30. *Corps Support Groups.* 17 June 1993.

FM 55-2. *Division Transportation Operations.* 31 January 1985.

FM 55-10. *Movement Control in a Theater of Operations.* 8 December 1992.

FM 55-12/AFM 76-6/FMFM 4-6/ OPNAVINST 4630.27A. *Movement of Units in Air Force Aircraft.* 10 November 1989.

FM 55-15. *Transportation Reference Data.* 9 June 1986.

FM 55-20. *Army Rail Transport Units and Operations.* 31 October 1986.

FM 55-30. *Army Motor Transport Units and Operations.* 14 March 1980.

FM 55-50. *Army Water Transport Operations.* 30 September 1993.

FM 55-60. *Army Terminal Operations.* 18 May 1987.

FM 55-65. *Strategic Deployment by Surface Transportation.* 10 May 1989.

FM 63-3. *Corps Support Command.* 30 September 1993.

FM 100-5. *Operations.* 14 June 1993.

FM 100-10. *Combat Service Support.* 18 February 1988.

FM 100-16. *Support Operations: Echelons Above Corps.* 16 April 1985.

FM 100-17. *Mobilization, Deployment, Redeployment, Demobilization.* 28 October 1992.

FM 100-19/FMFM 7-10. *Domestic Support Operations.* 1 July 1993.

FM 100-23. *Peace Operations.* 30 December 1994.

FM 100-27. *US Army/US Air Force Doctrine for Joint Airborne and Tactical Airlift Operations.* 31 January 1985.

FM 101-5. *Staff Organization and Operations.* 25 May 1984.

TB 55-46-1. *Standard Characteristics (Dimensions, Weight, and Cube) for Transportability of Military Vehicles and Other Outsize/Overweight Equipment (In TOE Line Item Number Sequence).* 15 January 1993.

Joint Publication 4-0. *Doctrine for Logistic Support of Joint Operations.* 25 September 1992.

Joint Publication 4-01. *Joint Chief of Staff, Mobility System Policies, Procedures & Considerations.* 15 September 1983.

Joint Publication 4-01.3. *Joint Tactics, Techniques, and Procedures for Movement Control.* 26 January 1994.

Joint Publication 4-01.5. *Joint Tactics, Techniques, and Procedures for Water Terminal Operations.* 16 June 1993.

PROJECTED PUBLICATIONS

These documents are projected to be printed for use with this publication.

FM 100-7. *Decisive Force Army in Theater of Operation.*

FM 100-8. *Combined Operations.*

FM 100-17-1. *Army Prepositioned Afloat.*

FM 100-23-1. *Foreign Humanitarian Assistance Operations.*

Joint Publication 4-01.1. *Joint Tactics, Techniques, and Procedures for Airlift Support to Joint Operations.*

Joint Publication 4-01.2. *Joint Tactics, Techniques, and Procedures for Sealift Support to Joint Operations.*

Joint Publication 4-02. *Doctrine for Health Service Support in Joint Operations.*

Joint Publication 4-06. *Joint Tactics, Techniques, and Procedures for Mortuary Affairs in Joint Operations.*

INDEX

By Order of the Secretary of the Army:

DENNIS J. REIMER
General, United States Army
Chief of Staff

Official:

Yvonne M. Harrison
YVONNE M. HARRISON
Acting Administrative Assistant to the
Secretary of the Army
00675

DISTRIBUTION:

Active Army, Army National Guard, and U.S. Army Reserve: To be distributed in accordance with the initial distribution number 110387, requirements for FM 55-1.

www.ingramcontent.com/pod-product-compliance
Lightning Source LLC
Chambersburg PA
CBHW080250290526
45790CB00005B/1759